By Jimmie Butler

Pursuing Timeless Agility
Deliver What Matters

PRAISE FOR DELIVER WHAT MATTERS

"Jimmie Butler offers more than a point of view—he provides a practical blueprint for restoring trust through delivery. By focusing on leadership posture over process, this book addresses the root of most transformation failures. It belongs on the desk of leaders who know their delivery model isn't working but haven't yet had the language to explain it."

Bill Pratt
Former Director, Enterprise Technology Governance – DHS
President, GovITWorks, LLC

"As a federal government product leader, I saw my world on nearly every page of this book. The patterns, constraints, and frustrations are real, and it names them with clarity and honesty. More importantly, it offers a practical path forward. If you're trying to lead products in government, this book will both validate your experience and challenge you to think differently about what it takes to deliver real outcomes."

Alonna Barnhart
Senior Federal Program Manager & Technical Advisor

"Over thirty years as a Contracting Officer, COR, and Program Manager, I have lived every failure mode this book describes. Butler names them with an accuracy that only comes from someone who has been accountable. This book belongs on every acquisition professional's desk."

Tonya Alston
Federal Acquisition Professional (30 years)
Author & Principal, The Alston Group

"*Deliver What Matters* is extremely valuable for leaders who already feel that something is broken but haven't been able to clearly articulate why. This book crystallizes a critical insight: while government excels at delivery, the next frontier is maximizing impact. It has meaningfully reshaped how I think about delivery, leadership, and the responsibility of service."

Ganesh Patil
President & CEO, Spectiva Group

"*Deliver What Matters* makes a compelling case for a new IT operating model. The five-posture framework stands out, giving leaders a clear, practical way to understand where they are and how to move forward."

John Binks
Former Chief, IT Management – DHS/FEMA
Technologist | Author

"Working inside a federal program, I've seen how much it matters that product ownership sits at the right level—close enough to understand the problem but empowered to make decisions. *Deliver What Matters* brings clarity to that reality and is especially valuable for leaders far removed from day-to-day delivery who still shape how it operates."

Loretta Carter
Federal Program Analyst and System Owner

"One thing consistently determines success or failure—whether the team truly operates as one. *Deliver What Matters* gets this right. It makes the case for a unified team focused on outcomes, with clear accountability and the authority to act. The ideas are practical, grounded, and long overdue."

Cass Panciocco
Former CEO, IntelliBridge

"*Deliver What Matters* reframes a truth many of us in GovCon have experienced but struggled to articulate: we're often busy delivering but not always delivering what matters. Jimmie offers a practical, leadership-driven blueprint for real mission impact. It's a must-read for GovIT."

Craig Baxter
VP Customer Operations, Improvix

"I found myself constantly nodding along—finally seeing the challenges I face every day clearly articulated. *Deliver What Matters* put language to what I've been experiencing and made it finally make sense. No matter where you sit in the system, it offers practical ways to start moving it forward."

Kirstin Tatagiri
Scrum Master, Government Contractor

"*Deliver What Matters* makes a compelling and deeply human case that trust is earned through what people actually experience, not just what institutions hope to provide. It's a thoughtful, practical, and timely contribution to the conversation about how government can work better for the people it serves."

Andrea Shields
Former GovCon Executive
Founder, Open Road Field Notes

"With rare honesty and clarity, *Deliver What Matters* says what most are afraid to. A must-read for anyone serious about transforming government IT from the inside out."

Roaa Mohamed
Enterprise Monitoring Lead, Agile Defense

"*Deliver What Matters* brings clarity to a frustration we all feel, but struggle to explain. It reflects a deeper issue in how value is delivered in government and offers a better way—one grounded in ownership, learning, and accountability. It's an approach I'd want to work in."

George Brewton
Software Developer, Government Contractor

Deliver What Matters

Deliver What Matters

Earning Trust by Redesigning
Government Digital Delivery

Jimmie Butler

Deliver What Matters
Earning Trust by Redesigning Government Digital Delivery
By Jimmie Butler

Stratēgi X

Published by StrategiX, LLC.
thinkstrategix.com

CONTENTS

OPERATIONALIZING THE SHIFT 147

FIGURES

FOREWORD

by Bill Pratt

There's an old saying that trust is built in drops and lost in buckets. In government and large enterprises, the same applies to our technology initiatives. Over the years, I've watched organizations invest significant effort into modernization, governance, and delivery improvements, only to find that public confidence does not rise at the same pace. The disconnect between effort and experience is real, and it has shaped many of the challenges I've seen inside large institutions.

As someone who has spent decades helping mission-driven organizations modernize their systems, I've seen how easy it is to drift back into old habits and how difficult it can be to pull a large institution back toward customer-centric, outcome-oriented work.

When I joined the Department of Homeland Security's (DHS) Office of the CIO, one of my first responsibilities was to assess why our systems were taking so long to deliver value. There was no shortage of skilled technologists or dedicated public servants. Commitment was not the problem. What we lacked was cohesion and clarity about outcomes. Teams were following dozens of different lifecycles, each designed to minimize audit risk rather than maximize user experience. We had optimized for compliance instead of trust. The result was that programs satisfied oversight requirements but failed to meaningfully improve the experience of the people we were meant to serve.

Over more than forty years in IT development, I've served as a test specialist, systems analyst, deputy department head, Section Chief, and Director of Enterprise Technology Governance at DHS. In that role, my team and I coordinated the adoption of the DHS Systems

Engineering Life Cycle and helped turn Agile from an experiment into the department's default approach for software development. We wrote the DHS Agile Development Guidebook, established Agile and Program Management Centers of Excellence, and supported a broad shift toward incremental delivery across the enterprise.

Those efforts moved the organization forward, but they also reinforced a lesson that has stayed with me—enterprise change requires constant attention. Personnel transitions, shifting priorities, and new delivery pressures gradually reshape how work gets done. Without reinforcement and leadership clarity, even the best improvements can lose their focus.

That experience is why I am excited about *Deliver What Matters*. Jimmie Butler has written more than another manifesto. He offers a practical blueprint for restoring trust through delivery. He reframes how leaders think about delivery itself, placing emphasis on who owns outcomes, how authority is distributed, and what it really means to lead when delivery is the mission. The guidance in this book works because it starts with leadership posture, not process. In my experience, that shift, more than any framework or method, is what determines whether change endures or collapses back into old habits.

Looking back, much of what I spent my career advocating for in GovIT is articulated here with a clarity I wish I had earlier. I had the benefit of hearing many of these ideas directly from Jimmie over the years, but what was previously conveyed through conversation is now codified in a way that makes the shift scalable. This book gives leaders the language and clarity that I did not have at the time.

One question Jimmie consistently asks his clients is deceptively simple: "Why should this program be funded?" He asks not to question the importance of the mission, but because too many programs struggle to explain how delivery connects to outcomes and public value.

In my current role advising companies that support government, that question has become unavoidable. Expectations around performance, outcomes, and return on investment are rising, and great delivery alone is no longer a sufficient answer. *Deliver What Matters* is aimed directly at that gap, offering a way for agencies and their industry partners to connect strategy to delivery in a way that justifies investment and sustains confidence.

This book belongs on the desk of leaders who sense that something in their delivery model is not working but have not yet had the language to explain why. It provides language for conversations that many organizations postpone and offers guidance grounded in real experience rather than theory alone.

My advice as you read this book is simple—do not treat this as a one-time read. Go through it once to understand the arc, then return to it as a reference for the work ahead. Share it with new hires and emerging leaders. In large organizations, memory is fragile, and a shared vocabulary is one of the few defenses against drift.

Building trust is not a side effort. It sits at the center of public service and enterprise leadership. Trust is earned through consistent, outcome-driven delivery and diminished when delivery becomes disconnected from impact. If you are prepared to examine how your organization defines success and who truly owns it, this book will serve you well.

Bill Pratt
Former Director, Enterprise Technology Governance, DHS
President, GovITWorks, LLC

INTRODUCTION

Confidence is lost in the gap between
what's delivered and what's needed.

Trust in government is shaped less by what leaders say and more by what people experience. It's formed by moments that rarely make headlines: applying for benefits, navigating a website, submitting paperwork, or waiting for a response. In those moments, government is judged not by intent, but by whether it works—whether it's clear, responsive, and capable of delivering what people need. Too often, it doesn't, and the consequences extend far beyond a single transaction.

The gap between effort and experience isn't the result of incompetence. Government is filled with committed public servants doing difficult work under real constraints. The issue runs deeper. It's a system problem. Work is structured, governed, funded, and measured in ways that haven't kept pace with rising expectations. As a result, even well-run programs can leave people frustrated.

In this book, "system" refers to the broader environment in which delivery happens—how decisions are made, how work flows, how authority is exercised, and how signals are used. Technology exists within that system, but it doesn't define it.

Over the past decade, agencies have invested heavily in improving delivery by modernizing platforms, adopting Agile practices, and expanding user experience efforts. These investments have improved how work gets done. Yet outcomes rarely improve systemically.

The reason is straightforward—the system is still organized around what's delivered more than what's achieved as a result. The consequence is erosion of trust for both the public and the internal users supporting them.

If you're responsible for how digital services are delivered in government—whether as an executive, program leader, product owner, or industry partner—this likely feels familiar. You've invested in better practices, modernized, and improved delivery. And yet, something still isn't connecting. The work is getting done, but the results are not consistently improving in ways that are visible, measurable, or trusted.

On one program I was advising, I brought together every federal and contractor staff member and opened with a sentence that immediately changed the temperature in the room. "We're not providing any value whatsoever."

The silence was deafening. Eventually, one federal employee spoke up. "I bust my butt day in and day out," she said, clearly perturbed. "Are you telling me I'm not providing any value?" "Correct," I replied.

Now with everyone's attention, I clarified my point. The team's effort, commitment, and competence were not in question. What I was challenging was the system we were operating within. Despite the volume of work and steady flow of deliverables, we were not creating value for the user or the mission in any meaningful, measurable way. We were productive by traditional standards, but not for our users.

That moment forced a much-needed conversation: What do we actually mean when we say "value," and how do we know when we've delivered it? This was our inflection point. The conversation shifted away from how much work we were doing toward whether any of it was making things better for the people we were supposed to serve.

It was around this time that I published *Pursuing Timeless Agility* to explain why Agile transformations were falling short. The struggle was not primarily within teams. It was that the system around them had not fundamentally changed. But even when Agile was practiced well, a deeper issue remained. Organizations often had not clearly defined which outcomes mattered, who owned them beyond delivery, or how improvement would be measured over time. No one was truly accountable for what was achieved as a result of what was delivered.

Deliver What Matters builds on that realization. This is not a book about Agile, user experience design, or delivery practices. Those matter, but they are well documented elsewhere. This book focuses on the system those practices operate within—how leadership decisions shape that system, and how that system determines what gets delivered and what gets achieved.

Nor does this book attempt to remove or ignore the external constraints that impact government delivery such as procurement, funding structures, and policy. These are real concerns that deserve a conversation and I hope this book sparks meaningful change there. But even within those constraints, organizations have more control than they often realize. Leadership decisions can still shape direction, ownership, and how learning influences what happens next. Leadership posture is where change begins.

In government, this shift doesn't mean adopting commercial models or chasing trends. It means changing how we think about what we build and manage. Digital services are not temporary outputs of projects. They are enduring assets through which mission outcomes are achieved. When they are treated that way, they are continuously owned, measured, and improved—not delivered and forgotten. This means redefining success in terms of user and mission impact, connecting strategy to delivery through signals, and creating operating models where outcomes are visible, ownership is clear, and learning is expected.

People don't judge government by what it intends to do. They judge it by what it actually delivers. Confidence returns when services work, when outcomes improve, and when progress is visible to those who depend on it.

Building trust through better delivery is both the challenge this book takes on and the opportunity it explores. This book is for those in government and industry who are no longer satisfied with activity as a proxy for progress—those ready to rethink how outcomes are owned and improved so that results, not effort, define success.

Section One

How Delivery Shapes Trust

Government has a trust problem. While politics plays a role, everyday digital experiences shape how people judge competence, care, and credibility. Trust erodes when those experiences fall short. This section examines how delivery models produce those experiences, and how the design of government digital delivery contributes to the trust deficit.

The chasm between government and the governed widens not just with policies, but with every click on a poorly designed interface.

CHAPTER 1

FAILED EXPECTATIONS

Trust rises or falls with personal experience.

Maria, a single working mom of two, had spent three hours on a Tuesday night applying for childcare assistance. The state's website was confusing, the forms were lengthy, and the application required her to submit a litany of documents she didn't understand or have readily available. Tired, frustrated, and stuck, she abandoned the website, took a deep breath, and got the kids ready for bed.

The next morning, she called the phone number listed on the website to see if she could apply by phone. After several attempts, she finally reached Daphne.

Maria explained what had happened the night before and asked if they could finish the application quickly so she could get to work on time. She'd been late a few times recently juggling changes in childcare. What Daphne told her next deflated her: "Unfortunately, everything you previously entered online was gone because there was no way to save or retrieve your progress."

Maria had to start over. This time, at least, someone could guide her through the application and explain what was needed. Even so, the process was still confusing. Thirty minutes later, Daphne completed the intake and gave Maria a list of supporting documents to submit by email. It took Maria two more days to gather everything required. That Friday morning, she scanned the documents, attached them to an email, and clicked Send—hoping she hadn't missed something important.

Inside the agency, Daniel, an adjudicator, worked through a growing queue of cases. By the time Maria's application surfaced for review, seventeen days had passed since she submitted her documents.

To review her submission, Daniel navigated between the primary case screen, a separate document viewer, and a compliance checklist. He opened attachments individually and cross-referenced required items against policy definitions, working methodically to ensure nothing was overlooked. One required document appeared to be missing.

Following procedure, he generated a request for additional evidence using a standardized template. The software populated the language, set a response deadline, and recorded the action. Daniel moved on to the next file.

Maria never saw the request. Two weeks later, she received a written notice stating that her case was closed due to insufficient documentation and lack of response. Her heart sank. Hoping for a better understanding, she checked the online portal. It simply showed the application as "Closed" without explanation.

Confused, she called the Helpline. After a 45-minute wait, she finally reached Michelle. Michelle confirmed that a request for evidence had been issued and that the deadline had passed. Frustrated and nearly in tears, Maria insisted she had submitted every required document. Michelle empathized, but there was nothing she could do. She could not see whether the uploaded files had been properly associated with the case record, nor could she reopen the case for further review. The workflow had moved on.

With no other option available, Michelle advised Maria to reapply. After five weeks, Maria was no better off than when she started.

From Maria's perspective, the system failed her. She did everything right and walked away empty handed. From Daphne's perspective, the application intake went as expected. She gave it no further thought. From Daniel's perspective, he followed policy and processed Maria's case efficiently. He noticed that her case dropped from his queue and wished for a better outcome, but he didn't have time to dwell on it.

From Michelle's perspective, she was constrained by what the software allowed her to do and carries deep empathy for Maria's plight. In each scenario, the application functioned as designed: it processed inputs, generated notices, enforced deadlines, and recorded activity. But it didn't deliver what mattered.

Maria needed clarity and confidence that her effort had been sufficient to gain childcare assistance. Daniel needed a program that surfaced complete information in one place to efficiently and accurately adjudicate Maria's request. Michelle needed visibility and authority to resolve discrepancies without sending Maria back to the beginning. Instead, each encountered friction inherent to the application. Taken together, those experiences communicated: *You don't matter here.*

> **The dilemma: Government programs are not designed to earn trust. They're designed to fulfill policy and regulation.**

Maria, the agency, and the characters in this story are fictional, but the experiences they represent are not. They reflect real patterns I've seen across government digital programs. When those patterns persist, the consequences show up in public trust. According to the Pew Research Center, only 17% of Americans in 2025 said they trust the federal government to do what is right "just about always" or "most of the time," down from 60% in 2001.[1]

Policy and politics play a role in that number, but this collapse in trust isn't driven by ideology alone. It's shaped by personal experience. Everyday interactions determine whether public services feel responsive, competent, and human…or cold, indifferent, and broken.

Evidence of unmet expectations exist inside government as well. The Federal Employee Viewpoint Survey (FEVS) and related workforce assessments regularly identify outdated technology and inefficient processes as barriers to effectively performing the job.

The bottom line is people don't trust what doesn't serve them well. They trust what works. They trust what listens. They trust what improves their lives. And yet, little by little, government loses trust through small, repeated, and avoidable failures.

If we want to build trust in government services, we have to stop treating trust as a messaging problem. It's not. Trust is a delivery problem, shaped by whether services work as people expect them to.

But before we talk solutions, we need to fully understand the problem we're trying to solve. This chapter explores how trust breaks down—not in scandals or headlines, but in the digital solutions people are forced to rely on every day. It begins a conversation government can no longer delay, one that demands an honest look at how digital experiences either build trust or insidiously dissolve it.

Trust Breaks Down at the Interface

For many people, a government website *is* the government. It may be the only interaction they have with an agency. If that experience is clunky, confusing, or unhelpful, they don't just question the service, they question the institution behind it.

For employees, the same dynamic applies. A case management application or help desk tool becomes their daily interaction with the organization. If those interfaces are inefficient and difficult to use, it shapes how they view leadership, priorities, and their own ability to serve effectively.

There was a time when people gave government a pass. Not because their experience was good, but because they didn't expect it to be. Frustration was accepted as the cost of doing business with bureaucracy. But that tolerance is disappearing.

Expectations are now shaped by modern digital experiences. The *Connected Government Report* found that visiting a government website is the most preferred way for people to access information and services, and that 75% of survey respondents expect the user experience to match or exceed leading private-sector companies.[2] People compare their interactions with government to the platforms they use every day—banking apps, retail portals, and delivery tracking tools. What they seek is clarity, responsiveness, and the ability to complete a task without confusion.

Employees carry similar expectations. They rely on internal platforms to process cases, manage workflows, and resolve issues. When those platforms require navigating multiple screens, reconciling disconnected information, or relying on manual workarounds, expectations go unmet. The software may technically function, but it doesn't feel effective.

For users of digital government tools, trust isn't destroyed because of a single breakdown. It erodes when the gap between expectation and experience appears repeatedly. At the interface, where people encounter government directly, trust is either reinforced or weakened. When experiences fall short often enough, confidence declines predictably.

Trust Erodes Through Experience

Think about what builds trust in a relationship. It's forged by knowing the other person is competent, reliable, and caring. You trust people who listen to your needs, follow through on commitments, and act with integrity. When someone fails to meet those expectations—or worse, doesn't seem to care—that trust erodes.

Trust in government works the same way. People want to be heard, respected, and valued. When they encounter obstacles, delays, or confusion, they interpret it as indifference. Eventually, apathy grows among users and the people trying to serve them. Skepticism replaces engagement. Over time, everyday friction—a glitch here, a confusing message there—accumulates into a pattern that suggests they are not the priority. And that pattern is backed by data. According to the 2022 *Connected Government Report*, just 17% of Americans said they believe the federal government cares about their experience. Only 19% said the same about their local government.[3]

According to McKinsey's *Public Sector Journey Benchmark Survey*, people who are satisfied with their experience are nine times more likely to trust the agency delivering it, and five times more likely to believe that public services are a good use of taxpayer dollars. That sounds like a great opportunity, but only 16% of Americans believe government has successfully used technology to improve service.[4]

Daniel and Michelle experience this every day. The tools and processes they rely on make it harder, not easier, to help applicants navigate the system. They're doing their jobs according to internal standards, but they're worn down a little more each time they cannot resolve an issue. When teams are dissatisfied with internal technology delivery, it can lead to "shadow IT," where business units take matters into their own hands seeking better solutions.

Trust isn't just a perception problem. It's a delivery problem.

Trust and experience are inseparable. When people feel ignored, trust erodes. When their needs are met with competence, reliability, and care, trust grows. But when erosion goes unaddressed, when no one is clearly accountable for fixing what's broken, frustration deepens into disbelief that government can improve at all. When that disbelief sets in, behavior changes—people disengage.

Disengagement Becomes the Default

When trust breaks down, it frustrates people and creates distance. Research by the Partnership for Public Service shows that when services fail to meet expectations, frustration turns to apathy.[5]

Disengagement becomes a self-reinforcing cycle. People who feel unheard stop speaking up. People who don't trust the program stop using it. People who feel like government doesn't care stop caring back.

Disengagement is a mission problem.

As trust goes, so does the government's ability to deliver on its mission. Disengaged users offer less feedback, are less likely to use digital services, and will interact with programs only when they have no other choice. Disengagement is a cascading failure that touches every part of government performance. The result is misaligned services, wasted investments, and more public frustration.

It plays out like this:
Poor service depletes trust → Mistrust increases costs → Higher costs delay improvements → Poor service continues.

The System Wasn't Built to Learn

Expectations aren't being met because the system doesn't enable people to own outcomes, learn, or improve within it. The operating model many agencies work within diffuses ownership for results, making it difficult to respond when services fall short. Ownership is spread across teams, vendors, and policy silos, leaving no one clearly accountable for the full experience.

The Childcare Assistance Improvement Program (CAIP) was responsible for building and maintaining the application Maria relied on. Alicia, the government lead overseeing the program, was accountable for delivering on commitments, managing program risk, and ensuring the application met expectations set by leadership. Requests flowed into CAIP, were translated into requirements, and delivered by the development team.

What CAIP didn't see clearly was how those decisions played out in practice. The problems Daniel and Michelle encountered every day rarely surfaced in a way that could change what was built next. Feedback existed, but it was fragmented, delayed, or disconnected from decision-making. The people responsible for improving the system were separated from the reality of how it was experienced.

This dynamic shows up in subtle but significant ways. Teams optimize for their portion of the process rather than the experience as a whole. Success is measured by compliance, delivery milestones, or contract performance, not by whether the service actually works for the people who rely on it. Feedback arrives late, if at all, and learning is optional rather than expected. When problems surface, they are escalated, documented, or handed off—but rarely owned.

Over time, the system adapts, but not in the way people hope. It becomes more proficient at managing process than improving outcomes. It reinforces controls and adds oversight, but what it doesn't consistently do is learn from friction in a way that prevents it from recurring. That reality exists despite the dedication of the people inside the organization.

Most government employees are deeply committed and work tirelessly to improve services, but commitment cannot overcome structure. When authority, measurement, and accountability are misaligned, improvement depends on individual heroics instead of institutional learning.

Unlike private firms, government agencies rarely face immediate market consequences when experiences fall short. Maria couldn't go to a different organization or use a different application method to apply for those state childcare benefits. Even if she could, the agency wouldn't register the loss as a problem—it would just be one less case to manage.

The absence of competition is not an excuse, but it removes an automatic correction mechanism. When breakdowns don't threaten program survival, they can persist longer than they should. Without structural ownership of outcomes, learning becomes incidental rather than inevitable. And when learning is incidental, expectations continue to go unmet.

Chapter Takeaways

Trust isn't shattered with a single incident. It erodes over time when people experience programs that feel indifferent to their needs and never seem to improve.

The takeaways below highlight the key drivers behind the trust gap:

- **Trust is earned through personal experience**: People don't separate trust in government from how it feels to use its services.

- **Expectations have changed**: People compare government experiences to the digital services they use every day.

- **Friction accumulates**: Small breakdowns compound into patterns that signal indifference.

- **Disengagement follows erosion**: When trust declines, people withdraw—reducing feedback, participation, and mission effectiveness.

- **Learning is incidental**: When ownership of outcomes is diffused, expectations go unmet because improvement depends on individual effort rather than institutional learning.

What's Next?

When we design services around the institution instead of the people it serves, we chip away at trust. Too often, those services aren't just ineffective—they're apathetic. The public feels it, and so do the employees trying to do better inside government.

This chapter explored how trust breaks down through everyday delivery experiences. Next, we'll examine why government services so often reflect institutional needs instead of individual needs, and what that reveals about how the organization is structured.

CHAPTER 2

BUILT FOR THE INSTITUTION, NOT THE INDIVIDUAL

Systems built for bureaucracy
rarely serve people well.

Most government services were not designed with trust as a primary goal. They were designed to administer programs, enforce policy, and manage risk. That orientation shaped how programs were built, how success was measured, and whose needs took priority.

Despite the usage data, people use government services out of necessity over loyalty. When usage is guaranteed, services don't need to compete for adoption. They only have to function well enough to process demand. The result is services that succeed by institutional standards but feel difficult and impersonal to the people who rely on them. It's not because teams don't care about users, but because the technologies they inherit were built to serve internal processes first.

That's why I often ask my government clients two questions:

- What if users had a choice?

- If they did, would they still choose your product or service?

For many leaders, this is the moment the conversation changes. They realize that use is not the same as success, and that activity metrics don't tell them whether the service actually works for people. It becomes clear that the operating model was never designed to win trust, but only to process demand. And once that realization lands, it's hard to unsee how deeply it shapes everything from requirements to timelines to how teams are rewarded for delivering.

That recognition hits because most teams already know it. It reframes service design as something more than merely meeting a mandate. It becomes about earning trust and delivering value that isn't just legally required but voluntarily appreciated.

Carolyn Colvin, Former Acting Commissioner of the U.S. Social Security Administration, captured this responsibility clearly:

> "Our customers don't have a choice when it comes to obtaining our services. They can't go to a competitor if we are not performing well, so we have an even greater responsibility than the private sector to provide a great experience."[6]

Colvin's point is more than an ethics consideration—it's a structural foundation. When users can't opt out, the burden shifts to the institution to earn trust through user experience instead of mission intent. That responsibility must be reflected in how services are designed, funded, governed, and measured.

In this chapter, we'll examine how institution-first design takes hold, how it undermines trust, and why good intentions alone cannot overcome systems that were never built with the individual in mind.

Built to Serve the System

When CAIP moved its benefits application online, the launch was framed as progress. The paper form was gone. The process was "modernized." Behind the scenes, the agency got exactly what it wanted: cleaner data entry, improved processing accuracy, and seamless integration with backend processes. This made Daniel's adjudication job easier, but for Maria, not much changed. The form was now digital, but it was still 19 pages long and no less confusing. She still needed Daphne's help to navigate the application.

> **When success is defined internally, experience becomes negotiable.**

Look at many government digital forms and you'll see the pattern: the workflow mirrors the underlying regulation almost exactly. Policy teams define the rules, legal teams interpret them, and Information Technology (IT) teams translate them into solutions. Each step is rational on its own, but together they produce services that reflect institutional logic rather than public understanding. This is how a simple digital form recreates, line by line, the same confusion and burden that existed on paper. The medium changes, but the experience doesn't.

In many agencies, no one is empowered to ask: *What's the experience like for the person on the other side of this?* The leadership model isn't built for that kind of accountability. It's built to minimize risk, ensure uniformity, and prove the agency met its mandate.

Once policy logic becomes the organizing principle, decisions drift away from how people experience the service. Improvements that don't map cleanly to policy are harder to justify, and changes that introduce ambiguity feel risky. Ultimately, preserving the structure becomes safer than questioning whether it still serves the people it was meant to help.

Government is Designed to Protect Itself

Organizations behave according to the incentives and risks embedded within them. Institution-first design persists because protecting the agency feels responsible. Those responsibilities matter, but eventually, the structures created to manage risk harden into an operating model where avoiding mistakes matters more than learning what works.

> **Risk avoidance becomes the design goal.**

That fear shows up everywhere, particularly in long approval cycles, rigid requirements, and overly prescriptive processes. Teams are trained to avoid failure rather than pursue impact, and the safest path forward becomes sticking to what's already been cleared.

The questions that dominate decision-making are predictable:

- Did we include every required policy field?
- Can we defend this decision to an oversight body?
- Will this avoid legal action?

And the questions that matter most lose priority:

- Can people understand this?
- Is this process faster or easier than before?
- Do users trust us more after using it?

When protection becomes the priority, users become collateral damage.

Internal Stakeholders Dominate Service Design

When services are defined, internal voices are almost always present. Policy, legal, procurement, security, privacy, and oversight all have seats at the table. Rarely is there an equivalent voice advocating for clarity, simplicity, or trust from the user's perspective. Each of these stakeholders brings legitimate concerns, but when their needs dominate the conversation, those concerns become design decisions.

This shapes how services are built. Individually, none of these needs are unreasonable as each exists to manage real risk. But together, they produce services that prioritize internal comfort over external clarity. The result is a digital experience where the content reads like legalese, workflows mirror policy diagrams, and the interface feels like paperwork in a browser.

The Culture of Safety Over Impact

Jeff, a contractor working at CAIP, was once told by a government manager that their top priority was to avoid negative press in the *Washington Post*. In that environment, change felt risky by default because every improvement introduced uncertainty, and every deviation invited review. The instinct became slow down, review more, stick to what's already been approved, ask for sign-off, and wait for consensus. Caution stopped being a response and became culture. Learning slowed, initiative faded, and improvement became episodic instead of continuous. Failure wasn't defined by whether Maria struggled to complete a process on her own. It was defined by whether the agency attracted oversight or negative media attention.

That kind of mindset emerges because the governance model teaches them what success looks like, and it becomes a filter for decisions. Most public servants don't wake up intending to frustrate users. But they are rewarded for avoiding errors, scrutiny, and surprises, not for improving experiences. That reward system shapes behavior.

Experience is the Evidence

By the time a service reaches the public, all the internal decisions are already baked in. What remains visible is not the intent, effort, or constraint, but the experience. The public doesn't see policy trade-offs or compliance decisions. They experience long forms, confusing instructions, and strict workflows. From the outside, those signals don't read as careful governance. They read as indifference.

People draw conclusions about competence, care, and credibility based on what they experience. Those conclusions progressively harden into stories they tell—and those stories shape trust.

This is the hidden cost of institutional self-protection. Governance models designed to shield the institution from risk inadvertently undermine the confidence they're meant to preserve. When user experience becomes evidence, trust isn't debated—it's decided.

Chapter Takeaways

The trust gap is rooted in a governance model that puts the institution's needs above the individual.

Here are the key barriers that keep government from earning trust:

- **Services are built to serve the system**: Government services often function as designed, but that design prioritizes policy and compliance over ease of use.

- **Institutional logic dominates service design**: Internal stakeholders set the requirements and IT implements accordingly, often without meaningful user advocacy.

- **Risk avoidance becomes the operating principle**: Teams are rewarded for minimizing audit exposure and risk over improving usability or mission outcomes.

- **User experience reflects internal priorities**: When programs are confusing, redundant, or indifferent, people don't assume complexity; they assume negligence.

What's Next?

The model described here was shaped by decades of decisions about how government organizes people, budgets, contracts, and risk.

In the next chapter, we'll look at the operating model itself, and how it prevents agencies from delivering services that earn users' trust.

CHAPTER 3

AN OUTDATED OPERATING MODEL

Delivery detached from ownership weakens results.

G overnment didn't set out to create an operating model that confuses users and demoralizes teams. But over time, that's what happened. What began as a way to control risk and manage work became a system that fragments ownership, obstructs learning, and disconnects delivery from outcomes. The very structure designed to ensure accountability and delivery excellence now prevents both.

In the last chapter, we looked at how services often reflect the structure of the institution more than the needs of the individual. But those user-facing symptoms stem from something deeper—an outdated operating model.

At the heart of this model is a pervasive mindset, that IT and software delivery teams exist to serve the business. This mindset is known as the Service-Provider Model, and it's ingrained into the way work is scoped, funded, delivered, and evaluated. This model doesn't just impact how work gets done, it defines who gets to shape it.

In this model, IT is treated as a vendor, even though it's internal. The business provides requirements and technology teams implement the solution. That might sound normal to you—expected even—but I think it's the root problem to solve. Within this model, even improved practices rarely lead to better experiences. The public is left with a government that can feel detached, despite the effort behind it.

IT Became an Order-Taker

In *A Seat at the Table*, Mark Schwartz describes a government IT culture that operates like an outsourced vendor, even to its own agency.[7] Having spent seven years as the Chief Information Officer (CIO) of U.S. Citizenship and Immigration Services (USCIS), Schwartz saw firsthand how IT was brought in only after key decisions were made. Their job was to build what was requested, not to shape what was needed. And no, those are not always the same thing. That setup reinforced a customer-service mentality instead of a problem-solving culture. It conditioned technologists to prioritize reactivity over relevance and scope fulfillment over strategic contribution.

This was the initial operating model at CAIP. Agency leadership funneled requirements into the program, the analysts translated them into detailed specifications, and the development team implemented them as requested. The people responsible for building the solutions were rarely involved in unpacking the problems they were meant to solve. The agency wanted the application form online, and it got it. Maria wanted a simple process she could complete on her own, on her time. She did not get that.

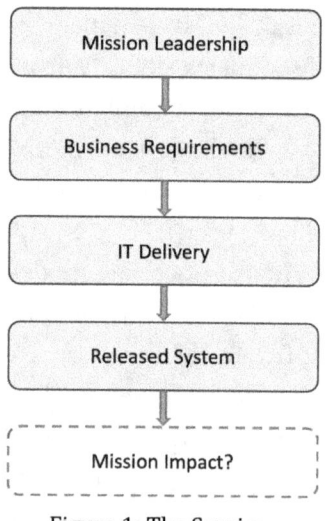

Figure 1: The Service-Provider Model

For historical context, the Service-Provider Model took root when IT was primarily responsible for internal infrastructure: servers, networks, and desktop support. In that context, a centralized, request-based model made sense, and still does. But as software became integral to how agencies deliver services, the same model persisted. Today, agencies are building user-facing digital products using a structure originally designed for managing utility services. That mismatch is now one of the biggest barriers to effectiveness.

This model emerged through a series of deliberate choices:

1. **Centralization**: IT functions were consolidated for efficiency, often into shared service models. That positioned them as fulfillment centers instead of strategic collaborators.

2. **Linear Project Planning**: Large-scale project models reinforced the illusion of predictability. Agencies locked in requirements, then handed them to IT for implementation.

3. **Compliance-First Culture**: Procurement, security, and policy restrictions defined projects before discovery even started. The focus shifted from solving problems to avoiding risk, often rewarding rigidity over responsiveness.

The result is IT teams trained to deliver outputs, not outcomes. They deliver efficiently, but they're rarely empowered to change course based on what they learn. Policy sets direction and delivery teams execute per requirements. Everyone plays a part, but clear ownership of results is often missing. That's how government IT can appear productive while still struggling to translate effort into meaningful impact.

Fragmentation Became the Norm

The operating model conditioned people around handoffs rather than sustained accountability for results. And it happened in four ways:

*   **Functional Silos**: Policy, IT, procurement, legal, and program offices each own a slice of delivery but rarely see the whole. The final experience reflects the structure of the agency rather than the needs of the individual.

- **Matrixed Oversight**: Authority is layered but not consolidated. Accountability for the full result is diffused. Everyone has a say, but no one is empowered to decide.

- **Role Misalignment**: Legacy job descriptions are shaped by sequential delivery models, where responsibility ends at the handoff rather than the outcome. Today's complexity demands integration, but most roles remain transactional.

- **Contract-Based Execution**: Delivery work is outsourced to vendors measured by scope completion rather than mission impact. Contractors are paid to deliver what's requested, not to challenge assumptions or advocate for the user.

This is how structure shapes behavior. These conditions discourage learning, limit decision-making, and make sustained ownership difficult to establish. Delivery teams build, policy teams approve, and design teams research, but there's little continuity from intent to execution to mission impact. And without continuity across the full lifecycle of delivery, even the best efforts become disconnected. Good intentions scatter across silos, leaving the user with services that meet delivery expectations, but are functionally disappointing.

New Language, Same Model

Despite embracing Agile, customer experience (CX), and digital modernization, most government IT shops still behave like service providers. While the terminology has changed, the operating model hasn't. Agile is often layered on top of old traditions. Teams may work in sprints with organized backlogs, but the work is pre-defined. Feedback may be gathered but it doesn't guide decisions. And delivery is evaluated by how fast it ships, not whether it solves the right problem. In practice, Agile often becomes little more than sequential delivery broken down into two-week sprints.

Organizations tend to measure what's easy to track: timelines, scope completion, and velocity. But those metrics say little about whether delivery improved the user experience or addressed the underlying mission problem. It's a classic example of the Streetlight Effect—we search for answers where it's easiest to measure instead of where they're most meaningful. In delivery, that ends up being outputs like features delivered because they're visible and easily counted, while outcomes go unmeasured.

Once a metric is introduced, it begins to shape behavior. That's the Hawthorne Effect at work—teams optimize for how they're measured. So, when teams are evaluated by velocity and throughput, meeting those measures become the goal, even when they reveal little about the effect of the work itself. The result is a delivery culture that rewards activity and predictability over insight and impact.

Product Leadership Is Constrained

Under the Service-Provider Model, product leadership rarely functions as intended. Decision-making authority is debated, ownership is scattered, and feedback is filtered through multiple layers before it can influence direction. Even when product roles exist, they operate within defined swim lanes that limit their influence on decisions.

In practice, product leaders are positioned to coordinate delivery rather than guide discovery or meaningful prioritization. They manage backlogs and facilitate execution, while decisions about scope, sequencing, and trade-offs are made elsewhere. Strategy is defined upstream, delivery is evaluated downstream, and product management sits in between with limited authority to influence either.

The result is not surprising. Teams manage roadmaps they didn't create. Research informs understanding but not decisions. Delivery is optimized for throughput and predictability, even when those measures provide no indication of whether the work improved the experience or produced results. Product leadership exists in title, but not in effect.

Contractors Are Considered Commodities

The Service-Provider Model impacts how agencies work with contractors, too. Jeff recalled being told during onboarding, "You're here to deliver client requirements, not to question them." Despite being hired for his product management expertise, his role was framed as passive execution. It signaled clearly, *you're here to deliver, not to define.*

Instead of being treated as strategic partners, contractors are often engaged like vending machines—paid to deliver requirements, with little room to question, adapt, or influence. That mindset isn't just discouraging, it limits how expertise can be applied, reinforces fixed assumptions, and narrows what delivery is allowed to address.

Jeff understood the users, their pain points, and the system constraints better than many of the decision makers tasking CAIP, yet his input was sidelined. Maria suffered the consequences because the experience was predictable and avoidable. After a while, people inside the program stopped trying to do better because it seemed futile.

Steve Jobs once asked: "Why hire smart people and tell them what to do?" In government delivery, that question exposes a structural tension more so than an individual leadership failure. Contractors are often brought in for their expertise, but the Service-Provider Model limits when and how that expertise can be applied. Decision authority sits upstream, requirements are fixed early, and delivery is evaluated by adherence to scope rather than contribution to understanding. As a result, specialized talent is used primarily for execution, even in complex knowledge work where learning and problem-definition are critical.

Contractors are expected to move fast but not rethink the path. They're expected to build to spec but not challenge whether the spec is right. This leads to a commoditization of contract labor. Agencies optimize for interchangeability, emphasizing plug-and-play roles and scope fulfillment over continuity, domain expertise, and learning. And those building the product are the furthest from the people who use it. Thus, feedback arrives late, context is missing, and learning is inhibited.

The Consequences of a Service-Provider Model

When IT is treated as a reactive service provider, the impact is not contained to delivery teams. It reshapes how the entire system performs.

Technologists are removed from problem definition. Decisions are made without full context. Work is executed, but outcomes are left to chance. Over time, this creates a pattern that's difficult to break. Effort increases, but impact does not. Teams stay busy, but progress becomes harder to see.

Inside the system, frustration grows. People who understand the problem are unable to influence it. Those responsible for decisions are too far removed from how the work actually behaves.

Outside the system, the experience deteriorates. Services become harder to navigate, slower to respond, and less aligned with what people actually need.

Nothing about this is accidental. It's the natural result of a model that separates delivery from ownership. And as long as that separation exists, improvement will be inconsistent—no matter how much effort is applied.

> **You can't build trust with an operating model that sidelines the people doing the work.**

Chapter Takeaways

The Service-Provider Model isn't named in process documents, but it's embedded in how work is scoped, funded, and measured. It shapes how requests are made, how teams are organized, and how success is evaluated—often without being questioned.

Under this model:

- **Technology is positioned as a fulfillment function**: IT is engaged after decisions are made, reinforcing execution over problem definition.

- **Ownership is fragmented across roles and approvals**: Responsibility is assigned, but no one is accountable for outcomes end to end.

- **Expertise is constrained by scope**: Both government staff and contractors are valued for delivery capacity more than judgment or insight.

- **Success is signaled by activity, not by impact**: Timelines, scope, and throughput stand in for evidence of improvement.

- **Teams are disconnected from users and mission outcomes**: Distance from real user experiences limits learning, accountability, and confidence.

These patterns persist not because people lack commitment, but because the operating model rewards predictability and control over signals and results.

What's Next?

The effects of this model extend beyond delivery mechanics. They shape how people working inside government programs experience their work, and how the public experiences government as a result.

In the next chapter, we'll examine how these structural limitations affect morale, engagement, and effectiveness inside government, and why internal experience and public trust are more tightly linked than many leaders realize.

CHAPTER 4

A DISCOURAGED WORKFORCE

Organizations that don't trust their people to
lead struggle to earn public trust.

The public isn't the only group frustrated with how government operates. Many employees inside government feel the same way. They're disconnected from decisions, disempowered to fix what's broken, and discouraged by persistent underperformance that rarely gets addressed. These frustrations don't stay internal. They show up in how services are delivered and how people experience government.

One clear example comes from a Department of Veterans Affairs study that found staff engagement is a leading predictor of customer satisfaction. Their conclusion was clear: "An engaged workforce is more likely to create a positive customer experience, resulting in higher trust."[8]

That finding shouldn't be surprising. When employees are asked to execute decisions that they did not help shape, and impeded by systems they cannot influence, something subtle but important happens. Ownership and initiative fades, leading to effort becoming compliance rather than commitment. In those conditions, service quality suffers, delays increase, problems linger, and feedback goes unanswered. And the public experiences not just inefficiency, but a lack of care.

This chapter shows how a discouraged workforce shapes public trust, and how the internal experience of government work shows up directly in the services the public encounters.

And the FEVS Survey Says…

Government is full of mission-driven people who care about the work and want to serve well. But when people feel their input doesn't matter, their expertise is dismissed, or their efforts are undermined, the result isn't just dissatisfaction—it's disconnection.

The Federal Employee Viewpoint Survey makes that clear. Its Global Satisfaction Index, which measures morale, motivation, and retention likelihood, stood at 65% in 2024. This reflects widespread strain in engagement across the workforce. Employees cited weak leadership, lack of recognition, and limited ability to make an impact as key contributors.[9]

Other findings reveal the cracks in day-to-day experience. Only 48% of federal employees said they are involved in decisions that affect their work. Many reported that performance, good or bad, makes little difference, reinforcing that effort and outcomes are disconnected.

The Impact of Unchecked Underperformance

Among the most discouraging forces in federal workplaces is unaddressed underperformance. According to FEVS, 40% of federal employees said that poor performers remain in their roles without consequences. Alicia faced this at CAIP. The process to remove a poor performer was arduous, taking nearly a year. In the meantime, morale eroded as the team saw poor performance persist. High performers disengaged, teams lost cohesion, and confidence in leadership waned.

When excellence is optional, apathy becomes contagious.

Within constrained operating conditions, managers often lack the authority, support, or incentives to address underperformance effectively. Over time, that reality sends a clear signal that effort and outcomes are loosely connected, shaping behavior across teams.

When employees stop believing their effort makes a difference, it shows up in how they deliver. And when the public encounters that apathy, trust in the institution declines.

Culture Shapes Behavior

Agencies often try to improve services through new tools, better processes, or updated performance metrics. But none of that sticks if the internal culture doesn't support accountability, autonomy, and purpose.

> **Culture shapes how teams behave when no one's watching.**

Culture determines whether people feel like contributors or cogs, and whether they're encouraged to lead or conditioned to comply. It fills the gap when priorities conflict, hard decisions must be made, or guidance is unclear. In those moments, culture—not policy—determines how people act.

In healthy organizational cultures, accountability is reinforced through expectations and signals rather than mandates. People are expected to think, to question, and to improve the work rather than simply execute instructions. Responsibility is paired with enough autonomy to act, and teams are held accountable not just for completing tasks, but for the quality and impact of what they deliver.

In unhealthy organizations, culture does the opposite. It rewards silence over initiative and compliance over discernment. Over time, people learn that the safest path is to follow orders, avoid risk, and stay within narrow lanes, even when they see opportunities to improve the service. That culture revealed itself when Jeff first joined CAIP. He recalled once sharing an idea and being told, "You're so cute with your enthusiasm, but that will never work. Nothing ever changes here."

When employees stop believing their voice matters, that indifference eventually shows up in the customers' experience.

Chapter Takeaways

The employee experience is one of the most overlooked drivers of public trust. When teams are ignored, disempowered, or operate in cultures that tolerate underperformance, the effects extend beyond morale. They shape service quality and influence public confidence in government itself.

This chapter showed that trust erodes from the inside out:

- **Trust is shaped internally before it's experienced externally**: When employees feel disconnected, that disengagement shows up in the services they deliver.

- **Morale reflects structural credibility, not just intent**: Only 65% of federal employees report satisfaction, signaling limited influence over decisions and direction.

- **Underperformance goes unaddressed**: 40% of employees report that poor performance carries little consequence, weakening confidence in accountability.

- **Disempowerment fuels apathy**: When teams lack context or voice, effort shifts from commitment to compliance.

- **Culture reaches the public**: A workplace that suppresses ownership produces services that feel indifferent.

What's Next?

This chapter exposed the hidden cost of overlooking the workforce. When employees stop believing their effort matters, the public begins to question whether government can deliver at all.

In the next chapter, we'll examine how these same structural limitations carry a steeper price—wasting time, resources, and opportunity in ways that compound frustration and erode trust.

CHAPTER 5

FAILURE COMPOUNDS OVER TIME

Unaddressed inefficiency multiplies system wide.

D espite widespread dissatisfaction, the demand for government services hasn't decreased. People still need benefits, permits, and other critical services. They just don't trust the systems delivering them.

It feels like a self-perpetuating cycle. Public distrust reinforces ineffectiveness, which, in turn, deepens skepticism. When government services are difficult to navigate, people lose faith in their efficacy.

As skepticism grows, so do operational costs. Staff must field more inquiries, teams must fix errors caused by poor design, and leaders funnel more money into short-term patches instead of long-term improvements. Every inefficiency and work-around drains resources that could have been invested in making services better.

These inefficiencies stem from how government IT often operates—as a reactive service provider responding to intake rather than as an owner of long-term service performance. The result is a reinforcing cycle: poor service increases operational burden, reactive spending diverts investment, and each round of short-term fixes deepens long-term inefficiency.

To understand how deeply this cycle is embedded, we'll break it down into three major forms of waste:

- **Operational Waste**: Unnecessary costs and inefficiencies from poor service design and complicated processes.

- **Investment Waste**: Money spent on redundant, ineffective, or underutilized platforms and services.

- **Mission Waste**: Failure to successfully meet policy goals.

Beyond wasting taxpayer dollars, inefficiencies weaken government's ability to achieve its mission. This chapter examines how these forms of waste compound over time, creating conditions where government steadily undermines its own effectiveness.

Operational Waste: The Cost of Inefficiency

Government serves millions of people through applications that should make service delivery simple. But when digital tools are poorly designed, they create friction that overburdens staff, increases support demand, and creates operational inefficiencies that carry financial, human, and mission consequences.

Here's how operational inefficiency compounds over time:

- **Increased support requests**: Confusing software forces users to seek help, raising call center costs and wait times.

- **Data entry errors**: Poorly designed forms cause mistakes that must be fixed manually, or impact adjudications.

- **Extended processing times**: Inefficiencies delay approvals and increase frustration.

- **Reduced staff productivity**: Complex workflows sap time and morale, pushing teams toward burnout or turnover.

- **Increased maintenance costs**: Short-term fixes and technical debt pile up, stalling progress and innovation.

These inefficiencies also have a hidden cost: declining trust.

Example: The Cost of Poor Digital Forms

An agency deploys an online form intended to streamline a critical service. But the experience creates more problems than it solves. Instructions are unclear, error rates are high, and users cannot easily complete submissions without help.

The impact shows up immediately. Applications are returned for correction. Call volumes increase. Staff spend time fixing avoidable mistakes instead of moving work forward.

What was meant to reduce effort adds to it. The system processes more work, but not better work. And the cost compounds with every submission.

Investment Waste: Spending Without Impact

Government agencies invest heavily in digital modernization, yet many projects fail to deliver meaningful outcomes. Instead of advancing the mission, they consume resources without improving results.

Poor investments do more than waste money. They also stall momentum, complicate operations, and crowd out better ideas, making it harder to recover even when problems are known.

In the private sector, bad products are phased out by market forces. But in government, projects persist long after their value fades. Agencies keep funding fixes and building around inefficiencies that rely on intuition over insight, even for declining user populations.

> The most expensive way to test an idea is by deploying code.

A Microsoft study found that most ideas fail to move the intended metric.[10] That's the cost of relying on intuition instead of data. Many of the ideas that came to CAIP were based on someone's personal belief that some change would be beneficial. But that belief wasn't formed from user feedback or evidence. Not surprisingly, the expected outcome was rarely achieved after deploying the requested change.

Commercial product leaders have long recognized that writing production software is the costliest way to validate an idea. Interviews, storyboarding, prototypes, and fast feedback loops offer a faster, and far cheaper, path to learning—one that reduces the risk of being wrong.

This is why so many government investments struggle. They proceed on intuition and spending continues even when value does not.

Here are a few ways poor spending choices create structural drag:

- **Operational strain**: Complex applications slow teams down and increase training and maintenance burden.

- **Misaligned spending**: Short-term fixes divert funds from improvements that could reduce long-term cost.

- **Redundant tools**: Siloed investments fund overlapping solutions, increasing support needs.

- **Opportunity costs**: Resources are consumed by low-impact efforts while mission-critical needs wait.

These are not isolated issues. They compound and erode confidence with every stalled rollout or underused tool.

Example: Investing in the Wrong Solutions

An agency launches a scheduling tool to improve field inspections. It's delivered on time and within budget, but it's built around internal reporting needs rather than how inspectors actually work.

Adoption stalls. Inspectors continue using spreadsheets. The tool remains in place, consuming millions in licensing and support costs, while the original problem—delays in scheduling and execution—persists. The investment is counted as a success. The outcome is not.

Mission Waste: The Impact of Falling Short

Government exists to serve its people. But when agencies spend more time fixing avoidable failures than advancing their objectives, trust takes a hit, and the mission suffers.

Poor investments divert attention, consume resources, and block agencies from advancing their objectives. As effort shifts toward rework and manual fixes, decision-making weakens, innovation slows, and public trust declines. Each failure makes recovery harder than the last.

Consider the impact of mission waste:

- **Ineffective service delivery**: Poorly designed applications prevent people from successfully accessing benefits.

- **Data & decision-making failures**: Low usability leads to incomplete or inaccurate data, limiting policy effectiveness.

- **Reduced operational efficiency**: Bureaucratic bottlenecks drain resources and slow progress across agencies.

- **Barriers to innovation**: Poor digital experiences erode support for investment, making change harder.

- **Erosion of public trust**: Consumers interpret poor service as incompetence, weakening the government's credibility.

Example: When Access Breaks Down

An agency launches a benefits portal intended to expand access. But without user input, the experience is confusing. Applications are abandoned. Eligible users fail to complete the process.

Staff are pulled into support. Backlogs grow. The people the program was designed to help are left waiting or never served at all. The system delivered a solution, but the mission did not move.

Chapter Takeaways

Government's ability to earn trust is undermined by a reinforcing pattern of waste—inefficient operations, misaligned investments, and missed mission outcomes.

This pattern shows up consistently:

- **Operational waste compounds quickly**: Inefficient applications burden staff, frustrate users, and raise costs without improving outcomes.

- **Investment waste hides in plain sight**: Spending prioritizes delivery and compliance over signals, usability, and mission fit.

- **Mission outcomes suffer most**: When effort is consumed by rework and fixes, progress toward real goals suffers.

- **Inefficiency reinforces distrust**: Poor service and public skepticism feed each other, locking agencies into cycles of activity without impact.

Until this cycle is interrupted, progress will remain expensive, fragile, and slow, and trust will stay out of reach.

What's Next?

Government has invested heavily in Agile, CX, and modernization. Yet the results remain inconsistent. The issue isn't effort. It's the model those efforts operate within.

> **You can't fix a broken system with the mindset that built it.**

That mindset is the focus of the next section. We'll examine why modern practices layered onto old assumptions haven't closed the gap, and what leadership looks like in a system not designed for outcomes.

WHY CURRENT APPROACHES HAVEN'T SOLVED THE TRUST PROBLEM

Widely adopted reforms promised to improve government delivery. Agile accelerated cadence. Customer experience sharpened insight. Digital transformation upgraded technology. Yet trust and user experience still suffer. This section looks at why these well-meaning reforms fall short, and what conditions must exist for them to deliver what matters.

Reforms promise improvement.

Structure determines results.

CHAPTER 6

AGILE ISN'T ENOUGH

Agile was never the destination.
It was meant to help us find the way.

Agile transformed how government teams deliver digital solutions. Popular frameworks are practiced widely across agencies, led by multi-certified professionals. Despite that, trust remains low, morale is uneven, and frustration with digital government services remains.

That evidence demonstrates that Agile isn't enough. But why? Is it because organizations aren't doing Agile properly? Is Agile the wrong approach for these organizations? Or is it because Agile, even when followed perfectly, falls short of what's truly needed?

For a time, Agile felt like the answer. It offered relief from robust requirements documents and promised more work and faster value through iterative and incremental delivery. It gave teams structure, rhythm, and a shared language for collaboration. But somewhere between the standups and the story points, the deeper purpose got lost. Some proponents argue that simply fixing how Agile is practiced is the answer. I disagree.

> Teams are moving faster, but not toward better outcomes.

Agile's real strength, its purpose, was never organizing delivery around what teams already knew or getting more things done quicker. It was about uncovering what they didn't yet understand—learning their way toward better solutions in complex environments.

Too often, learning has been replaced with delivery optics. Iteration becomes a delivery cadence rather than a learning loop, and velocity and predictability are mistaken for progress. Pivots happen, but they're more often reactions to pressure than adjustments informed by signals and supported by evidence. Pivoting becomes a badge of honor, often accompanied by the mantra, "At least we're Agile."

What Agile Was Meant to Be

Before Agile fueled the certification economy, it was a rebellion against spec-driven development. It challenged the assumption that requirements could be fully known upfront and that detailed plans guaranteed results. The early Agile pioneers weren't optimizing for velocity or predictability. They were searching for better ways to solve problems in uncertain, fast-changing environments where learning and adaptation mattered more than certainty.

The Agile Manifesto laid out values and principles, not practices and procedures. It emphasized human interaction over process, recognizing that collaboration solves more than contracts can anticipate. It prioritized working software over documentation because value lives in what users experience rather than what's written in a specification. And it valued responding to change over following a plan because no plan survives first contact with reality.

At its best, Agile is an approach to working:

- A way to uncover what works through feedback.

- A way to reduce risk by validating assumptions early.

- A way to evolve through continuous learning.

Agile brings humility to delivery. It accepts that we can't know everything up front. But Agile was never meant to define what to build.

It doesn't establish product vision, determine strategy, or decide how success is measured. That's not a flaw; it's an intentional boundary.

Many agencies crossed that threshold expecting Agile to deliver answers it was never designed to provide. The result is more output and more activity, without consistent evidence that the work improved outcomes.

What Agile Became

In *Pursuing Timeless Agility*, I described how Agile became distorted inside organizations that wanted the appearance of change without the disruption real change requires. To gain traction, early adopters made compromises. They sold predictability instead of adaptability, offering familiar comforts: fixed roadmaps, committed scope, and delivery dates that resembled what leaders already understood. Those compromises stuck. I called this the "unintentional intentional distortion of Agile."

Agile became Waterfall in a Scrum wrapper.

This distortion didn't happen because people were incompetent. It happened because they were under pressure. Leaders still needed to know what would be delivered and when. That hasn't changed. But Agile was never designed to guarantee certainty or deliver fixed scope on predetermined timelines. It wasn't intended to function as a project management framework, even though that's often how it shows up in government today.

As Agile scaled, what expanded wasn't learning; it was process. Frameworks promised coordination and predictability, but often at the cost of flexibility. Standardization replaced adaptation. Ceremonies multiplied while discovery shrank. Roadmaps hardened, planned program increments became immovable, and change became something to manage rather than something to learn from.

The result is a delivery culture that looks busy and polished but struggles to connect effort to outcomes. But no number of standups or retrospectives can fix an operating model that prioritizes predictability over impact. Agile isn't the problem—the system is.

Redefining Success

Most Agile teams are good at tracking activity. Story points, velocity, and burn-down charts provide a steady stream of data about how much work is getting done. What's far less common is evidence that any of that work improved outcomes for the user or advanced the mission.

That gap matters. When success is defined by delivery metrics alone, teams optimize for throughput rather than impact. They focus on completing work instead of validating whether the work made anything better. Outputs are easy to measure. Outcomes are harder, but they're the only thing that justify continued investment.

> **Value isn't in what you do. Value is in what is achieved as a result of what you do.**

Velocity and a smooth burn-down chart are not validation of delivered value. A faster build cycle doesn't mean a better product. A delivered feature doesn't ensure progress toward mission goals. When teams do not explicitly measure outcomes, success is assumed rather than proven, and delivery becomes the proxy for value.

This is how organizations digress. Features are delivered, tickets are closed, and programs stay busy, but the system never pauses to ask whether any of it changed the experience for the people it was meant to serve. Learning stops because nothing requires signals to translate into change.

Chapter Takeaways

Agile was created to help teams learn their way toward better solutions in uncertain environments. But it has often been reshaped to prioritize predictability and process over signals and results.

To understand why activity so often fails to translate into impact, agencies must recognize the limits of Agile:

- **Agile is a learning discipline, not a delivery model**: Its purpose is to generate feedback and guide adaptation, not to increase delivery activity or throughput.

- **Delivery activity is not proof of impact**: Agile can improve delivery cadence, but throughput metrics cannot show whether outcomes improved.

- **"At least we're Agile" is a warning sign**: Pivoting without signals and supporting evidence turns iteration into reaction and substitutes action for learning.

- **Scaling Agile often scales process instead of learning**: Frameworks can increase coordination, but they frequently harden roadmaps and limit discovery.

- **Value isn't delivered; it's realized**: Only achieved outcomes rebuild trust and justify continued investment.

What's Next?

Agile can help teams learn, but it can't decide what's worth learning or ensure insights lead to change.

In the next chapter, we'll look at customer experience, and why empathy, while essential, is not sufficient on its own either. Identifying pain points is only half the job. Turning insight into impact requires authority, ownership, and strategy.

CHAPTER 7

CX Isn't Strategy

*You can understand the user
and still build the wrong thing.*

Customer experience mandates have gained institutional support in government, reflected in the hiring of researchers and the creation of CX offices. According to a Deloitte survey, 81% of government managers say they're focused on improving CX and 70% believe their services are comparable to the private sector.[11] But user feedback tells a different story.

Despite the momentum, users still encounter confusing processes and disappointing digital tools. Agencies celebrate their research, but many users still feel stuck. The problem is that CX is often treated as an input instead of a driver. Agencies may observe the user, but they don't empower the people closest to those insights to lead the change. What looks like progress from the inside often feels frustrating from the outside.

The Illusion of Progress

When Executive Order 14058 was issued in 2021 and "America by Design" in 2025, it sent a clear signal of intent. Agencies responded with service design teams and more public research, but while internal metrics reflect activity and effort, external confidence remains low.

Independent benchmarks reinforce this gap. In a McKinsey customer satisfaction survey, government ranked last among major industries. Banks and credit unions topped this list with scores near 50, while traditionally low-scoring sectors like cable and satellite providers landed around 30. Federal government services, however, scored just 15—highlighting how far public-sector experiences lag expectations.[12]

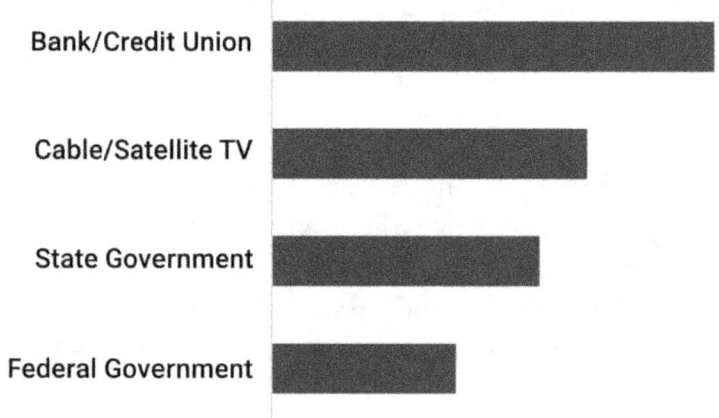

Figure 2: Industry Satisfaction Comparison
Source: Adapted from McKinsey State of States Survey (2022)

CX and design initiatives often yield tactical improvements such as redesigned forms and friendlier user interfaces, but they rarely address the conditions that create poor service in the first place. This isn't just a usability problem. It's a gap in how decisions are made and owned.

CX Isn't Positioned to Lead

CX teams play an essential role in understanding how government services are experienced. They identify pain points, surface usability friction, and advocate for empathy. But in many agencies, CX is positioned as an advisory function rather than a decision-making one.

CX sees the cracks. Someone else decides to fix them.

Teams can surface insights, but they don't have the authority to set direction. Research becomes disconnected from outcomes. Symptoms are understood, but decisions that address root causes sit elsewhere.

This separation is reinforced by how research is conducted. Access to public users is constrained by regulation. Feedback is often gathered in isolated moments rather than across the full experience. Responsibility for improving that experience is spread across programs, platforms, and vendors.

At CAIP, this limitation became visible when the team tried to engage directly with applicants to better understand where the experience was breaking down.

They could see the symptoms. Applications were being returned for correction. Call volumes were high. Adjudicators were spending time fixing issues that should have been prevented earlier in the process. But understanding why required seeing how people were actually navigating the application.

Access to users was not straightforward. Regulations limited how many applicants could be engaged and how that engagement could happen. Each interaction had to be structured, approved, and scoped in advance. Informal conversations—the kind that often reveal the most—were not an option. The team relied on indirect signals—call transcripts, adjudication notes, and limited research—to piece together what was happening, but the picture was incomplete.

Even when insights were clear, the ability to act on them was not. Decisions about what to change sat across multiple functions—policy, program leadership, and delivery teams—each with their own priorities and constraints.

The result was a familiar dynamic. Insight was available, but it did not consistently translate into coordinated change. The issue was not whether the team understood the problem. It was whether the system allowed that understanding to shape what happened next.

CX Needs Product Leadership

CX insight on its own does not change outcomes. It must be connected to ownership. In many agencies, that connection is weak or missing. Insight is gathered, but no one is accountable for turning it into decisions that shape what gets built and how it evolves over time.

Alicia and Jeff could see where the experience was breaking down. Even with constrained access to users, patterns were visible—through call transcripts, adjudication notes, and limited engagement. The signals were clear and often pointed to deeper issues than what had been requested. But acting on those insights required decisions that sat outside CAIP's control. What should change was visible. What could change was constrained.

> **You don't need more feedback. You need more ownership.**

Here's how CX and Product roles differ:

CX	Product
Surfaces pain points	Connects direction to delivery
Empathizes with users	Balances user and mission needs
Gathers insights	Prioritizes action
Suggests improvements	Owns outcomes
Measures pain points	Measures success

When product is missing, CX insights stay isolated. These insights are valuable, but untethered. Real impact only happens when someone is accountable for turning insight into decisions, and decisions into results.

Chapter Takeaways

Customer experience provides valuable insight, but without decision authority or ownership, those insights often fail to translate into better services or increased trust.

These takeaways capture why CX falls short as a standalone approach:

- **Public satisfaction still lags**: Despite CX investments, government ranks last across all industries in service quality.

- **Usability improvements are not strategy**: Fixing forms or workflows can reduce friction, but without clear product direction, impact remains local.

- **CX insights lack authority**: Research surfaces problems, but decisions about priorities and trade-offs are made elsewhere.

- **Ownership determines impact**: When no one owns the outcome end to end, insight accumulates but it doesn't lead to meaningful change.

- **Insight without action erodes trust**: Users feel the gap when government knows their pain but doesn't resolve it.

What's Next?

If understanding the user isn't enough, perhaps better technology is. Across government, digital transformation and modernization have become the great promise. Legacy applications are replaced. Platforms are upgraded. Infrastructure is strengthened. But new technical solutions do not automatically produce better outcomes.

The next chapter examines why modernization, despite its scale and urgency, often fails to restore trust, and what that reveals about how government defines transformation.

CHAPTER 8

MODERNIZATION ISN'T TRANSFORMATION

New technology can improve capability,
but only ownership improves outcomes.

F or decades, modernization has been the dominant response to government digital solution challenges. Agencies have migrated to the cloud, replaced legacy platforms, and implemented sophisticated deployment pipelines. Billions of dollars have been spent to upgrade infrastructure and refresh aging technology. These investments are not trivial. In many cases, they are necessary because aging platforms create operational and security risk while technical debt compounds. Eventually, replacement becomes unavoidable.

But modernization, however urgent, addresses capability. It does not automatically address outcome accountability. And when capability improves without a corresponding shift in ownership for outcomes, trust doesn't rise in proportion to the investment.

Modernization as a Reset

Large-scale modernization efforts rarely emerge from stability. They're typically launched when applications have reached a breaking point: when performance degrades, maintenance costs escalate, or risk becomes politically visible and the need for change is undeniable.

> **Modernization becomes the reset button for an application that was never designed to evolve.**

That pattern reveals something important. When an application requires wholesale replacement, it usually means it was not being continuously improved. It stagnated. Enhancements were deferred, user friction accumulated, technical debt compounded, and over time, incremental evolution gave way to complete overhaul.

In healthy product environments, major resets are rare because applications are continuously evolving to meet the mission need. Continuous feedback loops drive incremental adjustments. Signals surface emerging issues before they become crises. And ownership for outcomes facilitates continual enhancement to meet changing needs rather than periodic wholesale replacement.

Modernization at scale often signals that such ownership was absent. This is not a criticism of the teams managing those digital assets. It's a reflection of the operating model surrounding them. When delivery is funded as projects and measured by completion milestones, continuous stewardship becomes discretionary and deferred. Improvement competes with the next initiative for attention, and eventually, replacement becomes the only visible remedy.

The Project Pattern

Modernization programs are almost always structured as projects because they're big-bang, all-or-nothing efforts. They have defined scope, budget, and schedules, and produce tangible deliverables that culminate in a launch milestone.

CAIP was headed down this exact path. Agency leadership had decided to rebuild the existing application on a new platform while performing only minimal maintenance on the live system. The plan was to build the new application in full, launch it, and then decommission the legacy application.

Alicia and Jeff, the government and contractor lead, shared the same concern—Maria wouldn't see any real improvement for years while waiting for the new system to be fully built and deployed. They also knew that the odds of delivering what mattered through a large-scale, big-bang delivery were very low.

They explained to their leadership that if they waited years to deliver value while rebuilding the system from scratch, they weren't modernizing the service—they were postponing improvement and the chance to learn along the way.

Projects end. Outcomes do not.

When modernization is executed within a project paradigm, responsibility often dissipates at the point of deployment. The implementation team transitions off and attention shifts to the next initiative. Operational teams inherit the maintenance of the application but not the authority to refine it continuously in pursuit of outcomes.

The pattern is familiar:

1. A legacy application struggles.

2. Funding is secured for a replacement.

3. A new solution is built and deployed.

4. Attention moves on.

5. Obsolescence accumulates again.

Over time, that pattern reinforces the assumption that large-scale overhaul is progress. Projects succeed, but outcomes are disregarded.

The Illusion of Forward Motion

Modernization generates activity that looks like improvement: contracts are awarded, migration plans are executed, and milestones are reported. But from a user's perspective, the experience may feel only marginally better, or unchanged. From an employee's perspective, the workflow may still require workarounds. And from a mission perspective, performance indicators may remain static.

When visible investment fails to translate into felt improvement, skepticism deepens. People see effort, but they don't experience impact. Trust takes a hit not because modernization occurred, but because modernization didn't clearly improve what mattered.

This tension became difficult to ignore at CAIP. Jeff and Alicia saw how little changed for users despite ongoing effort. It raised questions about whether rebuilding the system would solve the problem or simply repeat it in a different form.

Continuous Evolution Versus Episodic Replacement

The difference between modernization and transformation becomes clear when you examine the problems they are designed to solve.

Modernization asks: How do we replace what's outdated?
Transformation asks: How do we change the conditions that allowed deterioration to persist?

> **Modernization upgrades platforms. Transformation upgrades the operating model.**

When outcome ownership is continuous, large-scale resets become less frequent. Feedback loops are active, performance is measured against outcomes, and continuous adjustments are expected. When those conditions are absent, stagnation accumulates until replacement appears to be the only viable solution. Modernization addresses the accumulated symptoms, whereas transformation addresses the operating conditions that allowed stagnation to persist.

Modernization itself is not the problem. In healthy systems, it plays a different role. Instead of periodic, large-scale resets, modernization happens in smaller, continuous increments—guided by signals, supported by evidence, tied to outcomes, and integrated into ongoing delivery. Capabilities evolve as needs change, rather than being deferred until replacement becomes unavoidable. The difference is not the technology. It's the operating conditions surrounding it.

This led to a different approach at CAIP. Instead of assuming wholesale replacement was the only path forward, the team began exploring how to improve the existing system incrementally, without the delay and risks of a full rebuild. It was still modernization but guided by outcomes, shaped by evidence, and integrated into ongoing delivery. That meant improvements reached people sooner.

Modernization Alone Cannot Build Trust

Trust grows when people experience improvement over time. It strengthens when services become clearer, faster, and more responsive. It stabilizes when someone is visibly accountable for addressing breakdowns. Modernization doesn't inherently produce those signals.

Technology can enable improvement, but it does not require it. Platforms can accelerate delivery, but they don't define direction. Automation can increase throughput, but it does not determine what matters. When modernization occurs inside a model that separates delivery from outcomes, new platforms inherit old disciplines. The infrastructure changes; the accountability does not. The result is predictable: improved capability without sustained improvement.

Chapter Takeaways

Modernization improves capability while transformation improves accountability. Conflating the two obscures why large investments in technology haven't consistently translated into improved trust or performance.

To understand why modernization alone is insufficient, agencies must recognize:

- **Modernization addresses accumulated technical debt, not outcome ownership**: Large-scale replacement often reflects years of deferred improvement rather than a culture of continuous evolution.

- **Projects conclude; outcomes persist**: Deployment milestones signal completion, not sustained performance improvement.

- **Visible investment does not guarantee felt impact**: Trust rises when experiences improve measurably, not when interfaces are merely replaced.

- **Continuous stewardship reduces the need for episodic resets**: When ownership for outcomes is clear, applications evolve incrementally instead of stagnating until replacement becomes unavoidable.

What's Next?

Agile changed how teams deliver. Customer experience insights sharpened awareness of users' needs. Modernization upgraded infrastructure and platforms. Yet trust remains fragile.

To understand why, we must examine how the operating model that governs these efforts strangles progress. In the next chapter, we turn to that constraint.

CHAPTER 9

THE CONSTRAINT BENEATH IT ALL

Learning without authority changes nothing.

Agile, CX, and modernization initiatives were introduced to help government deliver better services. Each promises improvement in its own way. Agile increases responsiveness, CX elevates users' needs, and modernization upgrades infrastructure and capability. In practice, however, each surfaces the same frustration: teams see what needs to improve but they operate inside a delivery model that cannot absorb learning or translate investment into sustained accountability.

Earlier chapters showed how Agile, without product leadership, becomes cadence without direction; how CX, without decision authority, surfaces problems that remain unresolved; and how modernization, without accountability, upgrades the platform but not the experience. This chapter looks beneath those patterns to name the shared constraint that limits them all.

The Pattern Beneath Failed Reforms

Agile, CX, and modernization each create visibility. Teams generate insight through retrospectives, research, analytics, and performance metrics. System performance becomes more transparent, pain points are documented, and technical limitations are exposed. But when it's time to act—when priorities must shift, scope must change, or investments must be redirected—authority often sits elsewhere.

Learning, investment, and insight accumulate, but ownership does not. Each reform increases capability to see the problem, but none of them guarantees authority to solve it.

> **When responsibility is distributed but ownership is unclear, improvement becomes discretionary.**

Government delivery is organized around distributed roles, where intent, execution, and oversight sit in different chairs. When outcomes fall short, responsibility is shared, but ownership is not. Rarely is a single leader empowered to respond end to end.

This condition is a byproduct of the Service-Provider Model. Success is defined by whether agreed deliverables are produced on schedule and within budget. Signals that may emerge during delivery are valuable, but inconvenient for meeting the prescribed metrics. Authority remains upstream, accountability diffuses across roles, and delivery continues even when it becomes clear that the work is not meaningfully improving outcomes.

Over time, energy shifts from progression to endurance. Software applications continue operating, but they don't systematically improve user and mission outcomes. Trust erodes not because effort is absent, but because improvement is confined by the operating model.

* * *

Agile, CX, and modernization exposed the real deficiency: no one owns outcomes end to end. Until authority and learning are held together, improvement efforts will repeat the same patterns. The next section explores what it takes to bring them together.

SECTION THREE

A NEW MODEL FOR GOVERNMENT DELIVERY

Good delivery is about building the right things and knowing they worked. It requires an operating model that can answer a simple question: Why should this program continue to be funded? This section introduces a Product-Led strategy as the choice to own outcomes through products. It shows how the Product-Led Model connects outcomes, product, and delivery into continuous improvement. And it defines the Leadership Operating System as what determines who gets to decide and whether learning changes decisions.

*Good delivery happens when
structure makes ownership
and learning unavoidable.*

How to Read What Comes Next

So far, you've seen the problem and why our current approaches are not solving it. We need another way. What comes next is not a set of new practices to adopt. It's a way to understand—and change—how delivery works.

To make sense of it, you need a way to see how the pieces connect. Here's that map. You don't have to understand all of this yet. Just see how it fits together.

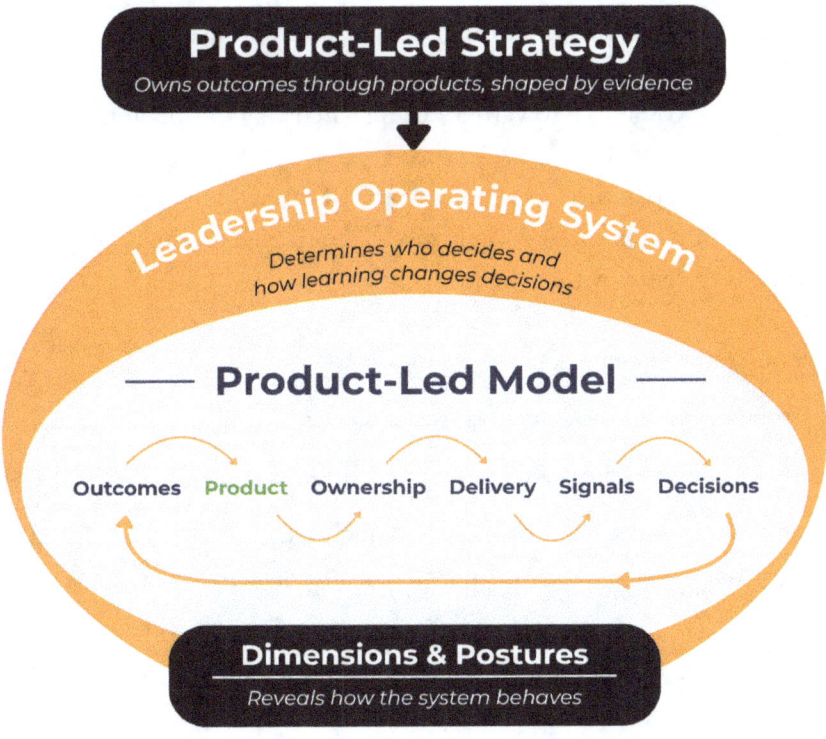

Figure 3: The Product-Led System

A Product-Led strategy is the choice.
It's the decision to move from delivering requirements to owning outcomes—treating products as the means through which mission results are achieved and improved over time.

The Product-Led Model is how that choice operates.
It connects outcomes, product, ownership, delivery, signals, and decisions into a continuous system—so that work doesn't stop at delivery but continues until outcomes improve.

The Leadership Operating System is what makes it hold.
It determines who decides, how decisions are made, and whether signals and learning change decisions.

The dimensions and postures show where you are.
They reveal how your organization behaves today and what progress looks like as you move toward a Product-Led way of operating.

These aren't separate ideas. They're parts of the same system. You don't implement them in order. You begin to see them, and then you start to operate differently within them.

As you read the next sections, ask:

- Where does ownership break down?
- What decisions are constrained, and why?
- What signals are visible, and which are ignored?
- Where does delivery stop short of impact?

Because once you can see those patterns, you can change them. And that's where the shift begins.

CHAPTER 10

THE PRODUCT-LED MODEL

Outcomes improve when the products behind them are continuously owned.

The Product-Led Model is not a process to follow. It's a system. In the interlude, you saw how the pieces fit together. This chapter brings that system into focus—how the parts connect to produce measurable improvement.

The Product-Led Model connects outcomes, product, ownership, delivery, signals, and decisions into a continuous loop. Products are not temporary outputs of projects. They are enduring assets through which mission outcomes are improved and measured.

In many organizations, delivery is organized around work that begins and ends. Projects are approved, requirements are defined, and solutions are delivered. Once complete, teams move on, and ownership diffuses. But the outcomes those solutions were meant to improve remain—persisting without clear ownership or sustained attention.

The Product-Led Model addresses this gap by shifting the focus from managing projects to managing products. Outcomes are pursued through products that are continuously owned. Delivery produces signals that reveal what's changing. Decisions adjust based on those signals, reinforcing what works and correcting what doesn't.

Not all work will present itself as a single, cohesive product. Small applications built on shared platforms are an example. But the model still applies. It clarifies where ownership must sit and what must improve, even when the boundaries are less obvious.

How the Model Works

The Product-Led Model is simple in structure but requires each element to function together. It's not a sequence of steps—it's a system in motion.

We'll walk through each element and how it contributes to the whole. Seeing how these parts connect is what makes it possible to recognize where the system is breaking down and what needs to change.

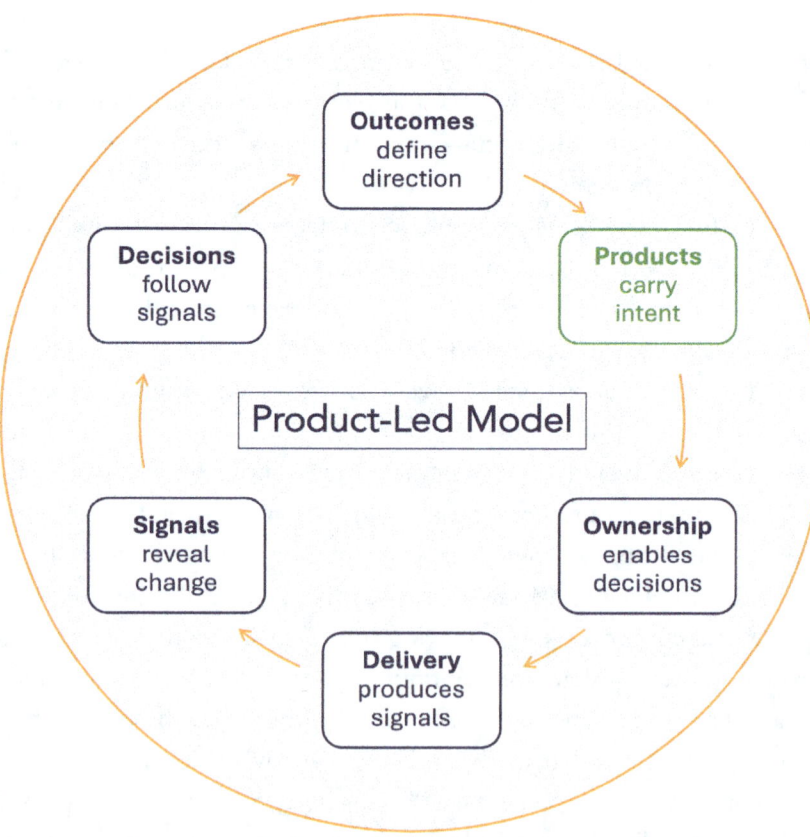

Figure 4: How the Product-Led Model Works

Outcomes Define Direction

Outcomes establish what improvement looks like. They define the condition the product is expected to change and how that change will be measured over time.

In many organizations, outcomes are treated as targets to achieve and move past. In practice, the conditions those outcomes represent rarely disappear—they evolve.

In the Product-Led Model, outcomes are continuously managed through the product. The product exists to improve those conditions over time, and its performance is measured by whether that improvement is happening. This changes how direction is set. Work is no longer defined by features or deliverables, but by the degree to which the product improves the outcome it's responsible for. When outcomes are clear and measurable, priorities focus, trade-offs become easier, and progress becomes visible.

Outcomes anchor the model. When they're disconnected from the product, teams deliver work but cannot determine if anything improved. When they're tied directly to the product, they establish the basis for ownership, delivery, and decisions.

Products Carry Intent

Products are the means through which outcomes are improved. They carry the intent of strategy into delivery and persist beyond any single initiative or release. Projects may begin and end, but the product remains. It continues shaping the user experience, influencing operations, and impacting outcomes long after delivery is complete.

In the Product-Led Model, products are treated as enduring assets. They're owned, measured, and improved because the outcomes they support do not end. Each decision and release contributes to how the product performs over time. This shifts how work is organized. Effort is no longer structured around isolated initiatives, but around improving the product itself. Delivery becomes a means of evolving the product, not completing predefined scope.

When products are treated this way, continuity emerges. Teams build context. Decisions reflect what's been tried, what's worked, and what hasn't. Improvement becomes cumulative rather than episodic. Without that continuity, the system fragments—work is completed, ownership resets, and outcomes drift.

Ownership Enables Decisions

Ownership establishes who's accountable for improving the outcome and who has the authority to act. That alignment enables decisions about the product.

In many organizations, responsibility exists without corresponding authority. Decisions require coordination, approvals, and escalation, creating distance between those closest to the work and those empowered to change it.

In the Product-Led Model, ownership is aligned to the product and persists. The team responsible for the product is accountable for the outcome it supports and has the authority to act within that context. This changes how decisions are made. Trade-offs are resolved closer to the work. Direction adjusts as conditions change. Teams act on signals instead of waiting for approval cycles to catch up.

When ownership is unclear, the system slows. Signals are observed but not acted on. Teams recognize what needs to change but can't make it happen. Ownership is what turns signals into action.

Delivery Produces Signals

Delivery is how the product evolves. Each change is intended to improve the outcome—but more importantly, it reveals whether that improvement is actually happening.

In many environments, delivery is measured by completion. Features are released, and work is considered done. Progress is defined by what was built rather than what changed.

In the Product-Led Model, delivery produces signals. Every change creates evidence about whether the outcome is improving. This changes how work is approached. Delivery is not only planned for implementation, but for validation. Assumptions are tested. Results are observed. Learning becomes part of the work, not something that happens after it.

When delivery is treated only as execution, signals are weak or absent. Teams complete work but lack clear evidence of whether it made a difference. Delivery provides the raw evidence the system depends on.

Signals Reveal Change

Signals make the effects of delivery visible. They show whether the outcome is improving. Metrics, user feedback, and operational data come together to reveal what's changing, what isn't, and where gaps remain between intent and impact. Over time, they create a shared understanding of progress.

Signals are not collected for reporting. They inform decisions. They show whether changes are producing the desired effect and where adjustment is needed. When signals are weak or misaligned, the system loses clarity. Teams continue delivering, but they cannot determine whether they are improving the outcome. Signals provide the visibility the system depends on.

Decisions Follow Signals

Decisions shape how the product evolves. They translate signals into action, determining what happens next and how the outcome is pursued.

In many organizations, decisions follow plans. Priorities are set in advance, and even when new information emerges, direction doesn't always adjust.

In the Product-Led Model, decisions follow signals. Evidence reveals what's working and what isn't, informing what to continue, what to change, and what to stop. This changes how direction is maintained. It evolves as evidence accumulates. Adjustments are made closer to the work, and the product improves incrementally over time.

When decisions do not reflect signals, the system disconnects. Delivery continues, but direction doesn't change. Effort accumulates without meaningful improvement. Decisions are what allow the system to adapt. They ensure that direction evolves based on evidence and that outcomes continue to improve.

What About Platform-Based Work?

At this point, a reasonable question starts to surface. This model fits large, cohesive applications such as public portals, case management systems, and internal tools used across the enterprise. But much of government work doesn't look like that.

A significant portion of delivery happens inside platforms. Teams configure workflows in ServiceNow, build automations in UiPath, and create applications in Salesforce. Requests come from across the organization. Work is delivered quickly and then the team moves on.

There's no single product. No unified experience. No obvious place for ownership to sit. It's easy to conclude that this model doesn't apply here. That conclusion is understandable, but incomplete.

Not Every Application Is a Product

Most of what gets built in these platforms is not a product. It's a collection of small, targeted solutions, each addressing a specific need. Treating each one as a standalone product creates artificial ownership and unnecessary overhead. Not every application should be treated as a product. But the solution those applications create still produces results.

Taken together, platform-based work shapes how something gets done—how long it takes, how much effort it requires, how often it fails, and how it feels to the people using it. That's the experience, even if no single application defines it.

The Model Still Applies—Just at a Different Level

Platform teams may not control mission outcomes. They don't define policy or manage operations in the field. But their work influences all of it. Cycle time. Error rates. Manual effort. Rework. Throughput. User friction. These are measurable changes in how the system behaves. Whether they improve or not is a result of what gets built, and why.

The Product-Led Model doesn't require every piece of work to become a product. It requires that the work connects to something that's being improved over time. Some work will remain small and transactional. That's not the problem.

The problem is when all work is treated that way—when nothing is expected to improve as a result. Even here, the question doesn't go away: Why should this work continue to be funded?

If the answer is activity, the model isn't in play. If the answer is mission improvement, something has changed.

Chapter Takeaways

The Product-Led Model shows how outcomes are continuously improved through products and the solutions they provide. It's simple in structure, but it requires consistency across each element.

- **Direction breaks down when outcomes are unclear or not measurable**: Without a defined condition to improve, work fragments and decisions default to urgency.

- **Products must be treated as enduring assets, not temporary efforts**: When they are not, ownership resets, signals are lost, and outcomes drift.

- **Ownership only works when it includes the authority to act**: Without decision-making ability, teams can see what needs to change but can't make it happen.

- **Delivery matters only when it produces signals**: Completing work without evidence of impact does not improve outcomes.

- **Measurement must reveal whether the outcomes are improving**: When metrics focus on activity instead of impact, they fail to guide decisions.

- **Decisions determine whether signals lead to improvement**: If direction does not change based on signals, the system is not operating as intended.

- **Not all work presents as a single product, but all work affects outcomes:** When improvement is not expected, delivery becomes activity without progress.

When these elements align, delivery improves. When they remain disconnected, progress stalls.

What's Next?

The model describes how delivery works. But understanding it is not the same as sustaining it. In many organizations, these behaviors break down under pressure—not because teams lack capability, but because the conditions around them don't support them. The next chapter shows what good delivery looks like when the system is working.

CHAPTER 11

WHAT GOOD DELIVERY LOOKS LIKE

Good delivery builds the right things
and shows, with evidence, that it helped.

G ood delivery is more than shipping work on time or launching a
new feature flawlessly. It solves the right problems for the right
people and delivers improvement the mission can feel. It connects
effort to impact in ways that can be seen and defended.

We've spent time examining what bad looks like: projects that
launch but don't help, teams that deliver but don't learn, and technology
that functions but doesn't serve. This chapter shifts the lens. Not
toward a theoretical future state, but toward something practical and
observable. If we're going to change how government delivers, we need
to be able to recognize when delivery is actually working well.

Recognizing Good Delivery

Good delivery is the result of conditions that make improvement
possible. You don't need a checklist to recognize healthy delivery, but
you do need signals. When delivery is working well, it shows up in how
problems are framed, how decisions move, and what improves.

> Good delivery is what a well-designed system produces.

In healthy delivery environments, teams can clearly articulate the problem they're solving and why it matters. They're not simply implementing requirements handed down to them; they understand the purpose behind the work and can connect it to mission impact. They understand how the product they are improving contributes to that impact over time, not just what's being delivered in the moment.

When new evidence emerges, direction adjusts without requiring a crisis to justify the change. Signals shape decisions in real time rather than being documented and ignored. Priorities are responsive. Decisions are made with context, close to where the work happens. Ordinary judgment calls don't get trapped in layers of unnecessary escalation. Work moves because those closest to the problem are trusted to act within clear boundaries.

Most importantly, users experience measurable improvement. The service becomes clearer, faster, more reliable, or more accessible. Something tangible changes, and that change can be observed, explained, and defended. These signals don't come from better tools or tighter oversight. They emerge when the system supports clarity, learning, and accountability as the norm.

When delivery is working well, these signals are hard to miss:

- Teams can clearly state what will change and how the product will improve as a result.

- Decisions move without waiting for escalation.

- Trade-offs are resolved close to the work.

- Direction adjusts as signals emerge.

- Work changes based on signals, not just what was planned.

- Improvements are visible in how the product performs for users, not just in delivery metrics.

The Conditions That Make Good Delivery Possible

When delivery works consistently, certain conditions are usually present. These are not aspirational values posted on a wall. They're structural realities that shape how work is framed and evaluated.

When the Product-Led Model is working, delivery consistently reflects:

- **End-to-end accountability**: Someone owns the outcome, not just the launch. They understand the problem, shape the response, and know whether it improved anything. Accountability doesn't dissolve at go-live.

- **Cross-functional problem-solving**: Policy, design, engineering, and operations work as one team. Context is shared, handoffs are minimized, and decisions reflect the full picture.

- **Continuous learning**: User insight, operational feedback, and performance data shape the work. Research is ongoing, and feedback changes direction.

- **Evidence-informed prioritization**: New information influences direction. Roadmaps organize intent—they don't lock it in.

- **Outcome-based success**: Progress is judged by what changed for users and the mission, not by how much was delivered.

When these conditions exist, delivery begins to feel different. Work is purposeful rather than reactive. Conversations center on impact rather than activity. And teams can explain not just what they built, but why it matters.

What Changes When Outcomes Are Owned

Government delivery is often judged by activity: *Did we launch the solution? Did we meet the deadline? Did we stay on budget?* Those questions matter as they protect resources and enforce discipline. But they don't answer the question that ultimately defines success: *Did it help?*

> **Shipping is an event. Improvement is the point.**

When success is defined primarily by outputs, accountability tends to end at launch. The project closes and the team shifts direction, but whether anything improved becomes unclear, or it becomes someone else's responsibility.

When outcomes are owned, the work is framed differently from the beginning—teams repeatedly ask a set of outcome-based questions:

- What problem are we solving?
- Who benefits if we solve it well?
- How will we know it made a difference?

These questions are practical filters. They shape scope, influence trade-offs, and determine whether a feature is worth building at all.

Owning the outcome does not guarantee that every initiative will succeed. Some ideas won't work as expected. The difference is that success is not declared prematurely, and signals are acted on—the results are owned and managed.

> **Teams need direction, not directions.**

One important signal becomes visible when outcomes are truly owned: teams don't wait for permission to make ordinary decisions. They operate with clear goals and guardrails and adjust when evidence changes rather than just working through a list of instructions. Where this exists, delivery accelerates without becoming reckless. Work remains anchored to purpose, and improvement becomes tangible rather than assumed.

Chapter Takeaways

Good delivery is recognizable. It produces visible improvement more than just visible activity.

When delivery is working well, you can observe:

- **Problems are clearly framed**: Teams understand what they are solving and why it matters.

- **Direction adapts to signals**: Evidence influences priorities without requiring crisis or escalation.

- **Accountability extends beyond launch**: Success is measured by improvement rather than completion.

- **Decisions move with context**: Ordinary judgment does not default to unnecessary approval cycles.

- **Users experience real change**: Services become clearer, faster, more reliable, or more accessible.

These are observable conditions. When they exist, delivery feels purposeful. Decisions make sense, progress becomes visible, and trust is strengthened through experience instead of promises.

What's Next?

This chapter answered a foundational question: What does good delivery look like? The next chapter defines Product-Led strategy—the strategic posture that makes this kind of delivery possible.

CHAPTER 12

FROM SERVICE PROVIDER TO PRODUCT-LED STRATEGY

When projects and requests drive decisions,
outcomes are accidental.

S trategy is often misunderstood. It's frequently confused with goals, initiatives, or roadmaps. Those are useful, but they are not strategy. Strategy is a set of deliberate choices about how an organization will pursue success. It guides how decisions are made when trade-offs are required and clarifies what will receive sustained attention over time.

A strategy has a reasonable alternative. A simple way to test whether something is truly strategic is to ask: Could a reasonable organization choose the opposite? If the answer is no, it may express an aspiration or value, but it's not a strategy.

For example, an agency might want to improve customer experience. But no reasonable organization would declare the opposite. That makes it an aspiration, not a strategy. A strategy requires a clear trade-off, something that's prioritized over other alternatives.

At CAIP, they chose to reduce the amount of time applicants needed to spend applying for and receiving benefits over optimizing for how efficiently it delivered incoming requirements.

The strategy of an organization becomes visible when priorities conflict or resources tighten. In those moments, leaders reveal what will be protected, what will be deferred, and what will be declined. At CAIP, that question began to act as a filter: How will this proposed change reduce the amount of time applicants need to spend in this process? Work was prioritized or rejected based on those answers.

Strategy is the pattern your decisions create. The distinction between declared intent and enacted trade-offs matters because digital delivery struggles when the underlying strategic posture doesn't align with the outcomes the organization claims to value.

The Service-Provider Model as a Strategic Posture

For decades, government has followed the Service-Provider Model. Responsibilities are clearly separated, and success is measured by responsiveness, compliance, and delivery against the plan. This posture is not the absence of strategy; it's a deliberate strategic choice.

The Service-Provider Model makes intentional trade-offs. It optimizes for predictability. It reduces ambiguity by separating mission objectives from technical execution. In stable environments with slower cycles of change, this model aligned well with funding structures, oversight expectations, and the pace at which technology evolved.

Like any strategy it optimizes for certain outcomes while deprioritizing others. The Service-Provider Model does not optimize for sustained outcome ownership. It does not assume that signals will reshape direction. Once requirements are defined and approved, delivery is measured primarily by adherence rather than by mission improvement—because that's someone else's responsibility. These are distinct choices for what not to do. It's the strategy.

But this separation creates distance between what is built and whether anything meaningful changed as a result. Completion becomes the dominant signal of success. Mission impact becomes harder to trace. The model fulfills requests efficiently, but it does not inherently steward long-term outcomes. This is the natural result of a strategic posture that prioritizes fulfillment over stewardship.

The Strategy Must Evolve

Digital services are no longer peripheral to mission execution. For many agencies, they're the primary way the public experiences government. Expectations are higher, complexity is greater, and policy, operations, and technology are tightly intertwined.

In this environment, a strategy that separates problem definition from delivery decisions becomes increasingly ineffective. When urgency or influence drives requests, delivery remains busy, but impact becomes difficult to demonstrate. Investments accumulate without a clear line of sight to improvement. Work is completed, yet progress is hard to explain beyond activity and compliance.

The issue is that the optimization target has shifted. Missions are more adaptive, users are less forgiving, and the platforms that support them must evolve continuously rather than periodically. Strategy must therefore do more than authorize work. It must guide judgment. It must clarify where authority sits, how signals influence direction, and who remains accountable for outcomes after launch. Without that alignment, delivery will struggle to produce consistent, meaningful improvement.

Product-Led as a Strategic Choice

A Product-Led strategy is a deliberate alternative to the Service-Provider Model. It's not a delivery methodology layered on top of existing structures. It's a strategic choice about how mission success is pursued and sustained. Where the Service-Provider Model treats technology as a fulfillment function, a Product-Led strategy treats products—digital capabilities—as enduring mission assets.

This shift began to surface at CAIP in how the online application was discussed. When it was treated as a tool to digitize application intake, requirements were grounded primarily in compliance. But as the program started to view the capability as an enduring product supporting user and mission outcomes, requirements began to be treated as assumptions to be tested rather than tasks to be completed.

A Product-Led strategy defines what is owned and why it matters. The Product-Led Model is how that ownership is exercised—connecting outcomes, products, delivery, signals, and decisions into continuous improvement.

A Product-Led strategy drives several intentional commitments:

- **Strategy functions as a decision filter**: Priorities are evaluated based on their expected contribution to defined outcomes rather than urgency or influence alone.

- **Accountability extends beyond launch**: Teams are responsible not only for delivering solutions but for understanding whether those solutions improved the problem they were meant to address—adjusting as needed.

- **Digital capabilities are stewarded as long-term assets**: Investment decisions consider durability, adaptability, and learning over time rather than simply completion of scope.

- **Signals influence decisions**: Assumptions are tested, feedback informs prioritization, and plans guide effort, but direction changes based on what signals reveal.

> **Product-Led refuses to separate delivery from mission accountability.**

Choosing to be Product-Led is therefore not a process adjustment. It reshapes how decisions are filtered, how authority is distributed, and how success is defined. It accepts that delivery and mission accountability cannot be separated without consequence.

Chapter Takeaways

The Service-Provider Model is a strategic posture—one that optimizes for predictability, role clarity, and fulfillment of defined requests. But today's delivery environment demands sustained outcome ownership and continuous adaptation to meet modern expectations.

To understand the shift from the Service-Provider Model to a Product-Led strategy, leaders must recognize:

- **Strategy is revealed under pressure**: What gets protected, deferred, or declined exposes the true priorities.

- **The Service-Provider Model optimizes for fulfillment, not stewardship**: It separates mission intent from delivery decisions and measures success by plan adherence rather than improvement.

- **Digital capabilities are enduring assets, not one-time implementations**: Without continuous ownership, completion replaces impact as the dominant signal of success.

- **Product-Led is a strategic choice, not a process overlay**: It keeps delivery and mission accountability bound together so learning alters direction and improvement compounds.

What's Next?

A strategic shift alone does not change behavior. If Product-Led is the chosen model, leadership must operate differently to support it. Authority, accountability, and decision-making patterns must reflect the strategy itself.

The next chapter introduces the Leadership Operating System required to make that alignment possible. It examines how leaders structure decision rights and accountability so delivery can consistently improve what matters.

Interlude: The Operating Model Shift

The difference between these approaches is not philosophical—it's structural.

In the Service-Provider Model, work flows through defined roles and handoffs. Requirements move forward, delivery completes, and responsibility resets. Whether anything improved is difficult to trace.

In the Product-Led Model, work is organized around products that persist over time. Outcomes, ownership, delivery, signals, and decisions are connected. Improvement is not assumed—it's measured and continuously pursued.

The shift is not in how work is delivered. It's in how responsibility is structured and how decisions are made.

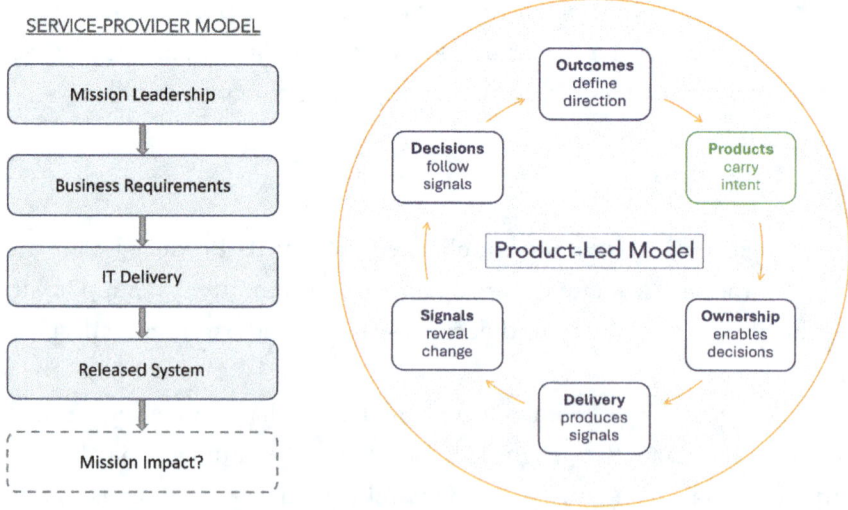

Figure 5: The Operating Model Shift

CHAPTER 13

THE LEADERSHIP
OPERATING SYSTEM

Strategy collapses when leadership
patterns contradict it.

An agency's CIO declares a strategic shift. After years of delivering under the Service-Provider Model, they announce a move toward a Product-Led strategy. Roles are formalized, objectives are set, and messaging reinforces the change: impact over output and ownership over fulfillment. On paper, the direction is clear.

Six months later, long-standing leadership patterns remain intact. Authority over meaningful changes still concentrates at higher levels. Significant decisions remain dependent on escalation. Performance systems continue to reward delivery against the plan more consistently than revision based on evidence. When direction shifts, it requires explanation rather than demonstration of improved impact.

Then a senior division chief role becomes vacant. Progress slows almost immediately. Teams hesitate to adjust scope, refine priorities, or make meaningful trade-offs until the position is filled. Work continues, but cautiously. Roadmaps are preserved rather than improved. No one wants to authorize a change that may later be reversed by their successor.

In another agency that also declared a Product-Led shift, a similar vacancy creates inconvenience but not paralysis because decision rights had already been clarified and transferred. Accountability for outcomes sits with teams rather than hierarchy. Guardrails are explicit. Within those operating boundaries, the work adjusts and moves forward. Leadership input matters, but it's not required for every consequential move.

The difference between these two agencies is not intelligence or commitment. It's whether the structure reinforces distributed authority and outcome ownership when conditions shift. That difference is the Leadership Operating System at work.

People behave according to the system they operate within.

A strategy announced from the top doesn't change behavior unless the operating model reshapes how decisions are made and sustained. This is not about personality. It's about structure—where strategy defines intent, and the Leadership Operating System determines whether that intent survives contact with reality.

Leadership Is a System—Not a Style

Most people talk about leadership in personal terms. They describe leaders as visionary or cautious, collaborative or directive. Style influences tone and personality affects presence, but neither determines how decisions move, how authority is exercised, or whether accountability persists through change. Systems do.

A Leadership Operating System is the structural design that governs how leadership functions day to day. It determines where decision rights sit, how accountability flows across roles and persists around the product, how direction is clarified, and whether signals and learning influence decisions. Every organization operates within one, whether consciously designed or inherited through habit and precedent.

Most Leadership Operating Systems evolve through governance routines, risk tolerances, promotion criteria, and the accumulated habits of prior leaders. Escalation pathways become normalized, approval layers solidify, and safeguards introduced for specific moments harden into fixed protocols. These patterns shape behavior more powerfully than any individual leader's stated intent.

> **Organizations reinforce what they measure, reward, and escalate.**

This is why leadership can't be reduced to personality. A leader committed to delegation inside a model optimized for control will struggle to enable autonomy. A leader committed to shared judgment inside a model that rewards escalation will still see decisions migrate upward. Conversely, when the structure supports clarity, distributed authority, and outcome accountability, continuity becomes more durable because the system reinforces the posture rather than resists it.

The Leadership Operating System is not defined on an org chart. It's revealed in how decisions move, how work adjusts, and whether accountability persists when conditions change.

When strategy and daily leadership patterns are misaligned, declared priorities yield to embedded behaviors. Teams optimize for what is reinforced rather than what is announced. That gap between intent and execution slows improvement and weakens credibility.

Understanding leadership as a system shifts the conversation. It moves the focus from individuals to structure and invites a harder question: What patterns are we reinforcing, and do they support the outcomes we claim to value?

The Dimensions That Shape Delivery

Leadership shows up in how work moves. Four dimensions most directly shape delivery: decision architecture, accountability over time, direction and constraint, and learning integration.

The contrast below shows how these dimensions behave in inherited systems versus Product-Led systems:

Dimension	Inherited System	Product-Led System
Decision Architecture	Authority defaults upward. Escalation is the norm.	Authority is aligned to context. Escalation is the exception.
Accountability Over Time	Accountability ends at delivery. Success equals completion.	Accountability persists to outcomes. Success equals improvement.
Direction and Constraint	Direction is prescriptive. Plans resist adjustment.	Direction defines intent and guardrails. Plans evolve with evidence.
Learning Integration	Learning is deferred. Signals rarely change plans.	Signals shape direction. Evidence informs priorities.

Decision Architecture

The first dimension of a Leadership Operating System addresses how decisions rights are structured.

Questions to answer:

- Where does authority reside?
- Which trade-offs can be resolved at the team level, and which must move upward?
- When uncertainty arises, is escalation the default response?
- How quickly can direction adjust when signals change?

In many inherited systems, authority concentrates up by default. Taking it up the chain of command becomes the safe response to ambiguity. This teaches teams that waiting is safer than acting because the structure reinforces caution over judgment.

In systems intentionally structured for delegation, decision rights are clarified rather than assumed. Leaders define purpose and operating guardrails and empower their teams. That authority carries expectation. Teams resolve competing interests within those clear guardrails, and escalation is reserved for matters that genuinely exceed delegated scope.

When meaningful adjustments require repeated permission from above, responsiveness slows and ownership weakens. When authority aligns with context, delivery becomes both faster and more accountable.

Accountability Over Time

The second dimension addresses the time horizon of accountability: who remains responsible, and for how long.

In project-based environments, accountability often ends at delivery when success is declared. Whether conditions improved for the user or mission becomes secondary, and someone else's concern. In Product-Led environments, that accountability is anchored to the product itself, not the effort that created it.

A different pattern is required when outcomes matter beyond deployment. Teams remain responsible not only for delivering capabilities, but for understanding whether those capabilities improved the mission metric they were meant to influence. Ownership persists through ongoing iteration beyond project completion.

If performance systems reward delivery against plan more than improvement against outcome, output-focused behavior will follow. If leaders consistently ask whether conditions changed rather than whether milestones were met, accountability deepens.

Sustained ownership depends on structure. Without it, delivery reverts to completion over improvement.

Direction and Constraint

The third dimension addresses how intent is established and how discretion is bounded.

Some leadership systems equate clarity with instruction, so detailed prescriptions are issued to reduce ambiguity. This means that plans are treated as fixed commitments rather than working hypotheses, and that deviations from the plan require approval because direction is interpreted as contractual.

Other leadership systems distinguish between intent and execution, so leaders define the problem to be solved, the outcomes that matter, the constraints that must be respected, and the measures that indicate progress. This means that execution decisions remain with those closest to the problem space.

When guidance is prescriptive, teams learn to seek approval before adjusting course. When intent and constraints are clear, teams operate within boundaries and refine their approach as evidence evolves. Judgment develops because it's expected.

When direction remains overly detailed, autonomy narrows and adaptation becomes cautious rather than continuous.

Learning Integration

The fourth dimension addresses how signals influence direction and whether new information meaningfully alters priorities.

In many inherited systems, plans become protected artifacts and deviation is treated as risk. Evidence that challenges assumptions triggers review rather than recalibration. Signals are acknowledged, but governance structures slow its influence because predictability is rewarded more than responsiveness.

In more adaptive systems, signals are expected to shape decisions. Assumptions are tested against real conditions, and evidence guides action rather than defending prior commitments. Learning becomes part of the delivery rhythm instead of an occasional correction.

When signals cannot meaningfully influence decisions, plans harden while reality continues to move. Over time, misalignment grows within a system that resists adjustment.

When Leadership and Strategy Align

Leadership turnover is a reality in government. Political appointments shift, senior executives rotate, and reorganizations reshape reporting lines. The question isn't whether it will happen, but whether authority and accountability are embedded deeply enough to withstand it.

Continuity during transition depends on where authority lives. When decision rights are tied to individuals, meaningful progress pauses. When decision rights are clarified, delegated, and protected by guardrails, work continues even as leadership changes. The difference is not confidence or competence. It's structural clarity.

CAIP experienced a leadership change at a critical moment during their shift toward Product-Led delivery. Under a different operating model, that kind of transition would have reset priorities, paused momentum, and forced teams to re-justify decisions already in motion.

That didn't happen. Decision rights had been clarified. Outcomes were already owned. Signals informed decisions, and progress was visible through shared measures. The new leadership didn't need to reestablish control—they just needed to be brought up to speed.

Every Leadership Operating System reinforces a posture. It either centralizes authority and protects plans, or it distributes authority and protects outcomes. It either ties accountability to events and titles or embeds it in roles that endure beyond any one leader. When leadership behavior aligns with strategy, continuity becomes reliable. When it doesn't, inherited habits override new intent.

> **The real test of a Leadership Operating System is not what happens when leaders are present. It's what continues when they are not.**

Chapter Takeaways

Every organization operates within a Leadership Operating System. It may be inherited or intentionally shaped, but it governs how authority, accountability, and learning function. A Product-Led strategy doesn't change behavior. It's enabled by the Leadership Operating System.

Strategy holds or collapses across four dimensions:

- **Decision Architecture**: Where authority sits and how decisions move.

- **Accountability Over Time**: Whether ownership persists beyond delivery.

- **Direction and Constraint**: Whether leaders clarify intent or prescribe execution.

- **Learning Integration**: Whether evidence reshapes direction or protects plans.

When leadership patterns and strategy diverge, behavior follows the pattern instead of strategy. When they align, delivery gains coherence.

What's Next?

Understanding the Leadership Operating System is not an academic exercise. It's a diagnostic lens. Once you can see how authority moves, how accountability persists, and how learning influences direction, a more practical question emerges: Where are we today?

Organizations rarely change how they deliver in a single step. Progress comes through deliberate adjustments to decisions, responsibilities, and ways of working. The next section introduces the dimensions and postures that shape those choices, helping you recognize where delivery stands today and what must change to produce stronger, more durable results.

Interlude: How the System Holds

The Product-Led Model describes how outcomes improve through products—connecting delivery, signals, and decisions into a continuous system. **The Leadership Operating System** determines whether that system functions. It shapes where authority sits, how accountability persists, and whether signals are allowed to change decisions. When these align, improvement becomes continuous. When they don't, the system fragments—delivery continues, but outcomes stall.

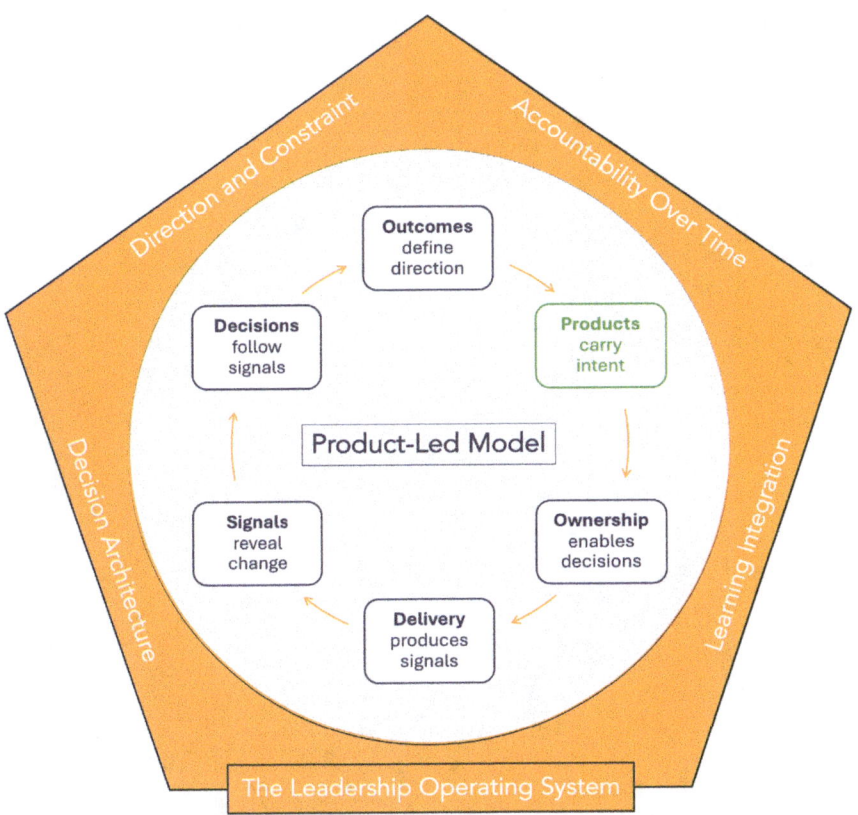

Figure 6: How the Leadership Operating System
Supports the Product-Led Model

SECTION FOUR

UNDERSTANDING THE SHIFT

Organizations rarely change how they deliver in a single step. Progress comes through disciplined adjustments to decisions, responsibilities, and ways of working—especially under pressure. The previous section defined how delivery works and what must be true for it to hold. This section introduces the dimensions that shape how delivery operates in practice and the postures that reveal how your system behaves. Together they help you recognize where delivery stands today and understand what must shift to produce stronger, more durable results.

Sustainable change is built
in layers, not leaps.

CHAPTER 14

SEE YOUR CURRENT STATE

You cannot outperform your own design.

P rogress does not begin with where you want to be. It begins with an honest reckoning of where you are and what your organization can realistically support. The version of your organization that matters is the one that shows up under pressure—when priorities collide, timelines compress, and leadership instincts take over. That's the version that determines what you can reliably sustain.

Many organizations make intentional choices when things are calm. The real question is what happens when those choices become difficult to maintain. That posture shows up in how work is prioritized, how authority is exercised, how evidence is used, and how leaders respond when delivery and outcomes come into tension.

How to Use This Chapter

The Product-Led Model describes how delivery works. The Leadership Operating System determines whether that model holds. The dimensions in this section help you see how your system behaves.

This chapter is not an assessment to rank your organization, or to label it as advanced or behind. It's a way to see your current delivery posture by observing how the system behaves when it's tested. Don't try to diagnose the entire organization. Look for where your system behaves one way in one area and a different way in another.

Pay special attention to:

- Where authority disappears under pressure.

- Where learning is welcomed—until it isn't.

- Where outcomes are discussed but not owned.

- Where governance reinforces intent or retreats to control.

The goal here is to gain clarity: a grounded view of what your system enables today, and what it cannot yet sustain. Subsequent chapters will walk you through the progression from one posture to the next. For a structured way to work through this with your team, see Appendix A.

The Five Dimensions of Product-Led Delivery

These dimensions reflect the conditions required for the Product-Led Model to operate. They describe whether your system allows you to own outcomes, preserve continuity, act on signals, make decisions close to the work, and hold intent when challenged.

Across each dimension, you'll see the same delivery postures:

- Reactive

- Tactical

- Deliberate

- Integrated

- Normalized

Your organization may be strong in one dimension and weak in another. That unevenness is normal. As you read this chapter, try to identify within each dimension where your delivery posture holds, where it breaks, and which constraints matter most right now.

Ownership and Accountability

Ownership answers a simple question: Who is accountable for the outcome and not just the work? Most people can describe who is responsible for delivery far more clearly than who owns the result.

Under Pressure: Who Owns the Result?

When priorities collide, ownership becomes visible. Watch what happens when a decision creates trade-offs. Does someone with real authority stay accountable for the result, or does responsibility spread across roles, dependencies, and process lanes?

How Ownership and Accountability Show Up:

Posture	What It Looks Like
Reactive	Accountability shifts as urgency rises.
Tactical	Accountability is tied to delivery commitments.
Deliberate	Ownership begins to shift, but it's still unstable.
Integrated	Ownership is clear and reinforced.
Normalized	Ownership is explicit and sustained.

Reactive

In a reactive posture, accountability shifts as urgency rises. Work is thrust into the team like a fire drill. Leaders intervene because no one is clearly empowered to own results. Responsibility spreads across teams.

Tactical

In a tactical posture, accountability is tied to delivery commitments. Teams deliver what was requested and leadership coordinates. Accountability is defined by commitments instead of impact. This posture can deliver reliably, but it cannot adapt intentionally.

Deliberate

In a deliberate posture, ownership begins to shift, but it's still unstable. Problems are discussed before solutions are selected and teams better understand the purpose behind the work. Someone is accountable for defining success and tracking progress. Deliberateness introduces outcome ownership, but it doesn't guarantee its resilience.

Integrated

In an integrated posture, ownership is clear and reinforced by governance, roles, and decision rights. Leaders focus on removing obstacles and empowering the team. Outcomes are defined and have clear owners with the authority to make decisions. Trade-offs stay with the owner instead of being managed elsewhere by default.

Normalized

In a normalized posture, ownership is explicit and persists through organizational change. Outcomes are owned by default and ownership endures because it's encoded in roles, expectations, and decision-making structures. Failure still happens, but it's visible, owned, and learned from rather than deflected or obscured.

Why Ownership and Accountability Matters

Without clear and stable ownership, delivery may become more efficient, but effectiveness remains constrained because no one is positioned to adjust direction when results fall short. Work continues to ship, yet signals and learning remain disconnected from decisions.

Funding, Contracts, and Continuity

Funding and contracting determine what your organization can sustain long enough to learn. The challenge is not only how much funding exists, but how predictable it is and how it's structured—does it support continuity of outcome ownership.

Working Within Constraints

Funding and contracting are often treated as fixed boundaries. While the Federal Acquisition Regulation (FAR) defines those boundaries, leaders still have meaningful leeway within them.

Funding models that reward completion over improvement reinforce the patterns organizations are trying to change. But delivery can still be guided by evolving outcomes, even when contracts emphasize defined deliverables. It's extra work, but it can be done.

Meanwhile, there's a conversation that must continue—one that aligns procurement, funding, and delivery around stable teams and evolving outcomes. Until then, leaders must work within current constraints while deliberately shaping them where possible.

Under Pressure: What Gets Sustained vs Reset?

Pressure exposes whether continuity is designed or accidental. Look at what happens when funding tightens, oversight increases, or a vendor transition begins. Does the system preserve domain knowledge and decision ownership, or does it reset measures and direction by default?

How Funding, Contracts, and Continuity Show Up:

Posture	What It Looks Like
Reactive	Resources shift rapidly to address urgency.
Tactical	Contracts reinforce execution against commitments.
Deliberate	Funding and contracts allow signals to shape decisions, but continuity remains vulnerable.
Integrated	Funding and contracts reinforce enduring ownership and support decisions based on signals.
Normalized	Continuity is sustained, and contracts consistently support ownership and decision-making.

Reactive

In a reactive posture, resources shift rapidly to address urgency. Work is often supported through short-term adjustments, reprogramming, or stopgap measures. When urgency subsides, attention and resources move to the next hot spot. Learning is rarely carried forward, so similar issues reappear later, often with greater cost and frustration.

Tactical

In a tactical posture, contracts reinforce execution against commitments and performance expectations. Contracts reward scope adherence, predictability, and delivery pace. Signals may exist, but they have limited influence once plans harden. Teams execute well, but direction remains governed by intake and inherited priorities rather than evidence.

Deliberate

In a deliberate posture, funding and contracts allow signals to shape decision occasionally. Even that level of continuity, however, can be unstable. When organizational dynamics change, expectations can quickly revert to execution-first behavior. Deliberate funding allows signals to influence decisions, but it does not yet protect them.

Integrated

In an integrated posture, funding reinforces enduring ownership and outcome accountability. Performance expectations evolve as understanding deepens. Contracts reinforce accountability for outcomes, not just activity. Together, funding and contracting create continuity, allowing ownership and learning to compound over time.

Normalized

In a normalized posture, contracts allow continuity to persist across budget cycles, leadership changes, and vendor transitions. Teams expect to revisit assumptions, refine success measures, and evolve solutions over time. Learning compounds because it's no longer situational. It's embedded in how the system operates.

Why Funding, Contracts, and Continuity Matters

Funding and contracts are leadership signals about what matters. Without continuity, ownership cannot endure and signals cannot compound into evidence. Even when outcomes are clearly owned, contracts and incentives that prioritize delivery speed over evidence force teams back into execution-first behavior. Execution may improve, but the system keeps paying to relearn what it already knew.

Measurement and Learning

Measurement reveals what a delivery system truly values. Not what it claims to value, but what it consistently reviews, rewards, and allows to influence decisions. Signals shape what gets attention, and over time, what gets attention is what gets protected.

Under Pressure: Do Signals Change Decisions?

Most organizations can produce signals. Fewer allow them to change decisions when they create discomfort. That discomfort reveals whether evidence has authority or merely visibility. When signals challenge assumptions, do they trigger inquiry and adjustment, or does the system defend the plan and treat them as a threat to commitments?

How Measurement and Learning Show Up:

Posture	What It Looks Like
Reactive	Signals are gathered ad hoc to explain or defend.
Tactical	Signals track performance and plan adherence.
Deliberate	Signals inform learning, but influence is inconsistent.
Integrated	Signals connect effort to impact and inform decisions.
Normalized	Signals consistently shape decisions and direction.

Reactive

In a reactive posture, signals are gathered ad hoc and retrospectively in response to incidents. Measurement feels burdensome, disconnected from daily work, and rarely influences what happens next. Teams learn that data is something to defend with, not something to learn from.

Tactical

In a tactical posture, signals track delivery performance and plan adherence. They provide predictability and control, and deviations are treated as risk. Signals that emerge late are often deferred because commitments have already been made. Teams can see that work was delivered, but not whether it mattered.

Deliberate

In a deliberate posture, signals begin to shape decisions, but influence is inconsistent. Outcome measures appear and begin to inform local decisions, but under pressure, delivery metrics often crowd out impact signals. Deliberate measurement enables insight, but it does not yet ensure that decisions consistently reflect it.

Integrated

In an integrated posture, signals connect effort to impact. Data is trusted, timely, and actively used to inform trade-offs. Teams rely on it to improve both how work is done and what work is chosen. Signals reinforce accountability, and decisions change because the system expects it and governance supports it.

Normalized

In a normalized posture, signals shape direction by default. Success criteria are explicit, revisited, and refined as understanding deepens. Evidence challenges plans without triggering defensiveness. Learning compounds because insights are retained, shared, and acted on even as people and priorities change. Measurement is no longer used to prove success. It's used to improve it.

Why Measurement and Learning Matters

Without meaningful signals, delivery becomes aimless repetition. Learning is a leadership choice, reinforced by what is measured, reviewed, and allowed to change direction. What your organization pays attention to determines what it's capable of improving.

Team Authority and Decision Rights

Authority determines whether teams can do more than just execute. It's about placing decisions as close as possible to the information needed to make them well. When decision rights are unclear, teams wait for direction, follow instructions, and delegate uncertainty upward. Leaders, in turn, become decision bottlenecks.

Under Pressure: Where Do Decisions Get Made?

Authority is rarely revealed by org charts. It shows up when a team needs to make a real trade-off: scope vs. timeline, risk vs. learning, output vs. outcome. Observe where the decision lands. Does it stay with the team, or does it move up by default as soon as uncertainty appears?

How Team Authority and Decision Rights Shows Up:

Posture	What It Looks Like
Reactive	Decisions escalate immediately as urgency rises.
Tactical	Teams decide how to deliver, not what or why.
Deliberate	Authority expands but can revert under pressure.
Integrated	Decision rights are clear and reinforced.
Normalized	Authority is explicit and exercised consistently.

Reactive

In a reactive posture, decisions escalate immediately as urgency rises. Teams wait for direction as leaders step in to make decisions directly. Teams learn not to act unless explicitly instructed. Abdicating decisions is the safest path, and learning is deferred in favor of immediate relief.

Tactical

In a tactical posture, teams decide how to execute assigned work, but not what to deliver or why. Scope, priorities, and success criteria are defined elsewhere. Teams optimize for execution. Signals are acknowledged but rarely allowed to change direction once plans are set.

Deliberate

In a deliberate posture, authority expands, allowing teams to participate in problem framing. They can test assumptions, adjust plans, and respond to signals, but authority is often conditional and may retract when tension rises. Deliberate authority enables inclusion, but it does not yet guarantee influence.

Integrated

In an integrated posture, decision rights are clear and reinforced. Teams accountable for outcomes are also empowered to make the decisions necessary to achieve them. Leaders focus on alignment, and decisions stay close to the work without losing coherence across the organization. Authority remains stable under pressure because it's supported by governance, incentives, and leadership behavior.

Normalized

In a normalized posture, authority is explicit and exercised consistently. Teams are inherently trusted to make decisions within their domain. Decision rights persist across organizational changes because they're encoded in roles, expectations, and operating norms. Teams act decisively because they know where authority lives, and leaders consistently reinforce that clarity.

Why Team Authority and Decision Rights Matters

Misaligned authority collapses accountability and suppresses learning. Leaders compensate by intervening more frequently, and teams respond by minimizing risk. Delivery may be efficient, but adaptation becomes increasingly difficult.

Authority isn't about relinquishing control. It's about placing decisions where they can be made well and sustained over time.

Leadership Behavior and Governance

Every organization has moments when stated intent is tested: a delivery slips, a metric declines, or a stakeholder escalates. In those moments, leaders choose whether to reinforce the operating system they're trying to build or revert to behaviors that feel safer and more familiar.

Under Pressure: Does Leadership Reinforce Intent?

Leadership is tested when stakeholders escalate, delivery slips, or outcomes are questioned. In those moments, leaders teach the system what matters most. Watch for the reflex. Do leaders protect intent and ownership, or do they bypass the system to restore speed and certainty?

How Leadership Behavior and Governance Show Up:

Posture	What It Looks Like
Reactive	Leaders intervene directly to resolve issues.
Tactical	Leaders reinforce plan adherence and compliance.
Deliberate	Leaders invite learning, but behavior varies when stakes are high.
Integrated	Leadership behavior consistently reinforces intent.
Normalized	Leadership sustains learning regardless of who leads.

Reactive

In a reactive posture, intervention dominates. Leaders step in frequently to make decisions, resolve issues, or redirect work. These interventions often resolve short-term issues, but they teach the system to wait for direction. Teams learn that relinquishing decision rights is safer than ownership, and signals are deferred in favor of immediate relief.

Tactical

In a tactical posture, leaders reinforce plan adherence and compliance. Leadership behavior emphasizes predictability and control, relying on reports, checkpoints, and reviews to maintain alignment. Variance is risky and signals that challenge direction are ignored rather than explored. Teams become skilled at meeting expectations, but not at questioning assumptions.

Deliberate

In a deliberate posture, leaders ask better questions and create space for signals and evidence. They focus on outcomes rather than tasks and decisions rather than explanation. That behavior, however, is not yet consistent. Under scrutiny, leaders may revert to familiar controls. Teams learn to read cues, adjusting how they surface uncertainty. Deliberate leadership invites signals, evidence, and accountability, but it does not yet protect them.

Integrated

In an integrated posture, leadership behavior is consistent and reinforcing. Leaders protect outcome ownership, support learning, and remove restrictions rather than absorbing decisions themselves. They focus on strengthening the system rather than bypassing it. The organization learns that intent holds even when outcomes are uncertain because leadership behavior is predictable and aligned.

Normalized

In a normalized posture, leadership sustains learning regardless of who's in the room. Leaders are evaluated on how well they enable outcomes instead of how tightly they control execution. New leaders adapt to the system rather than reshaping it around preferences. Over time, leadership behavior becomes a stabilizing force. Intent is no longer dependent on individual leaders; it's institutionalized.

Why Leadership Behavior and Governance Matters

Leadership is the ultimate constraint. When leadership reverts under pressure, the system follows, regardless of what the teams are doing well. Conversely, when leaders consistently reinforce intent, even imperfect systems can improve.

Leadership and governance are not about control. They're about creating the conditions where good decisions can be made repeatedly. Without aligned leadership behavior, no operating model can endure.

* * *

The Product-Led dimensions describe what good delivery requires. But they are enabled—or constrained—by how leadership operates.

The Leadership Operating System defines how decisions are made, how accountability persists, how direction is set, and whether signals influence decisions. These conditions determine whether teams can own outcomes, whether funding supports continuity, whether decisions can be made at the right level, and whether signals actually change direction. Ultimately, a Product-Led shift succeeds or fails based on the Leadership Operating System. We'll explore that next.

Coach's Note

It's easy to overestimate your organization's posture. But the worst thing you can do is define a starting point that's further along than you really are.

That's what CAIP was doing before Jeff, the contractor lead, joined. They were trying to do too much, too soon, and the result was predictable: nothing changed. The ideas were there, but the ability to execute fell short.

That explains the pessimism Jeff encountered when he began discussing new ways of working. When people said, "nothing changes here," they weren't being cynical—they were speaking truth from experience.

I know I said earlier that this isn't a maturity assessment and I encouraged you to avoid ranking yourself that way, but it's hard not to—I get it. No one wants to admit to being "less mature." Whatever your assessment though, it's not personal. You didn't create those conditions, you inherited them, so own it—humbly.

The purpose of this chapter is not to judge where you are. It's to help you stop guessing and start seeing your system as it actually operates so that you can move forward in a way that's responsible and that will stick.

THE EVOLUTION OF DELIVERY CAPABILITY

Delivery capability evolves through a series of recognizable shifts. Each stage changes how decisions are made, how authority is exercised, and how signals and learning influence direction.

Across the next chapters, we'll examine how delivery systems progress.

Reactive → Tactical
Control emerges

Tactical → Deliberate
Judgment enters

Deliberate → Integrated
The system aligns

Integrated → Normalized
The system internalizes

Each transition strengthens the system's ability to choose well, adapt to reality, and ultimately deliver what matters.

The chapters that follow explore how leaders make each shift hold.

CHAPTER 15

FROM REACTIVE TO TACTICAL

Reactive delivery absorbs disruption.
Tactical delivery stabilizes it.

Reactive delivery exists when urgency becomes the organizing principle. Work arrives faster than it can be shaped, and everything feels like an emergency, so priorities are negotiated in real time. Decisions are made to relieve pressure rather than to improve outcomes. The teams stay busy, leaders stay involved, and the system survives, but it does not improve.

Firefighting becomes the standard operating procedure as teams struggle to keep up with a flurry of ever-changing urgent requests. Commitments shift faster than ownership can stabilize, decisions are revisited repeatedly as conditions change, and the system loses the ability to choose deliberately. Even capable people operating with good intentions find themselves reacting rather than choosing. They want to break the cycle, but the system keeps pulling them back into reaction.

That constant reaction has a cost. When urgency dictates every decision, the system loses the ability to shape work thoughtfully. As a result, stability feels out of reach, and improvement feels secondary to short-term relief.

In the pages that follow, we'll examine the leadership decisions required to replace reaction with structure, so that urgency no longer dictates how work enters the system and how commitments are made.

Orienting the Transition
Reactive → Tactical

The shift from reactive to tactical delivery is a shift from impulse to intention. Urgency does not disappear completely, but it no longer dictates every decision.

In a reactive posture, requests arrive faster than they can be assessed and decisions are made for comfort rather than for shared commitments. There's no basis for which to prioritize or deny, and escalation becomes routine because ownership never stabilizes.

A tactical posture introduces executional discipline. Intake is filtered, priorities are sequenced, and roles are clarified. This leads to work becoming more predictable because commitments are shaped before they are accepted. But the discipline is bounded. Direction is still decided by intake patterns, stakeholder urgency, and inherited priorities. Tactical delivery strengthens execution, but it does not yet redefine what is pursued.

By reducing reaction, the structure creates space for decision. That's crucial because, without decision, no meaningful response is possible.

How Reactive and Tactical Delivery Show Up:

Signal	Reactive	Tactical
Commitments	Made under duress	Shaped before acceptance
Ownership	Diffuse or unclear	Anchored to delivery
Learning	Incidental	Retrospective
Authority	Pulled upward	Assigned for execution
Behavior	Firefighting dominates	Problems stay within roles

Establishing Tactical Discipline

Moving from reactive to tactical delivery is not about fixing everything at once. It's about introducing just enough structure to replace chaos with coordination.

Minimum Viable Tactical

Progress at this stage depends on a few conditions holding consistently:

- Work intake is shaped before commitments are made.

- Roles and responsibilities are clear enough to understand where decisions are made.

- Delivery commitments are stable enough to plan against.

- Leaders reinforce predictability rather than reacting to noise.

These changes do not improve outcomes or enable learning. They prove that the system can replace reaction with coordination.

Tactical delivery solves a specific problem: unpredictability. Requests are evaluated for viability and fit before they become obligations, work is ordered more intentionally, and delivery stabilizes to support forecasting. Delivery commitments begin to hold.

But tactical delivery does not yet govern direction. While work becomes more predictable, direction is still largely decided by intake demand pressure. The delivery system may execute predictably but it's not guaranteed to deliver what matters.

The risk at this stage is complacency.

Predictability feels like progress because it restores control. But coordination is not strategy, and execution discipline is not outcome ownership. Tactical delivery must be treated as a starting point rather than an end state.

Three Common Misreads:

- **Improved execution equals improved outcomes**: Work becomes more predictable, but impact remains unchanged.

- **Coordinated planning equals strategic clarity**: Priorities are sequenced, but direction is shaped by intake and urgency.

- **Predictable delivery equals learning capacity**: Discipline improves reliability, but evidence has not gained authority.

Tactical delivery creates stability. What the organization does with that stability determines whether it becomes merely reliable, or deliberately adaptive.

How This Transition Manifests Across the Five Dimensions

Tactical delivery first appears in execution. Stability begins to form in how work is shaped, assigned, and reinforced. The following dimensions reveal where tactical delivery is taking hold, and where reactive habits may still persist.

Ownership and Accountability

In reactive delivery, accountability crumbles under pressure. Tactical delivery reintroduces it but limits it to only delivery commitments.

What Changes Here:

- Accountability stabilizes around delivery commitments.

- Teams are accountable for execution; leadership is accountable for coordination.

- Escalation decreases as ownership becomes clearer.

Accountability is tied to predictability, but it remains output focused. Outcomes may be discussed, but ownership for results is still unclear, creating awareness without creating stewardship.

Funding, Contracts, and Continuity

In reactive delivery, funding responds to unforeseen urgency. Tactical delivery stabilizes funding and contracts around planned execution.

What Changes Here:

- Contracts reinforce execution against defined commitments.

- Performance prioritizes predictability over learning.

- Teams experience continuity long enough to plan but not to adapt direction.

Stability enables coordination, but it still restrains learning. Contracts reward delivery adherence more than insight, and direction remains largely fixed once commitments are made.

Measurement and Learning

In reactive delivery, signals are gathered ad hoc and retroactively, often in response to urgent data calls. In tactical delivery, signals track execution against plan, though data calls persist.

What Changes Here:

- Signals track plan adherence and delivery performance.

- Status discussions replace post hoc justification.

- Variance becomes visible earlier, but impact remains unclear.

Tactical measures reduce chaos, but they do not yet explain impact. Signals exist around delivery execution, but they rarely influence direction once plans are set.

Team Authority and Decision Rights

In reactive delivery, teams escalate decisions because they must. Tactical delivery gives teams authority to execute, but not to choose.

What Changes Here:

- Teams decide how to deliver assigned work within defined commitments.

- Scope, priorities, and success criteria are defined elsewhere.

- Authority becomes clearer but remains tightly bounded.

Efficiency improves, but adaptability doesn't. Teams execute well but are not yet empowered to question assumptions or shape outcomes.

Leadership Behavior and Governance

In reactive delivery, leaders intervene to relieve pressure. Tactical delivery shifts leadership behavior from intervention to oversight and guidance.

What Changes Here:

- Governance emphasizes plans, commitments, and variance.

- Leaders intervene less frequently in day-to-day execution.

- Control shifts from personal intervention to procedural oversight and guidance.

Stability increases, but compliance can begin to overshadow inquiry. Signals and evidence that challenge direction may be managed cautiously to avoid disrupting delivery.

If This Feels Familiar

If urgent requests regularly reshape priorities and decisions are made to relieve pressure rather than improve outcomes, you may still be operating reactively.

If the system is calmer than it used to be, but a lot of time is still spent negotiating priorities, you may be showing early signs of operating tactically.

If leaders are relieved that chaos has receded but are hesitant to disturb what's finally working, you may be protecting coordination more than progress.

If you're seeing these patterns, tactical delivery is present. It's real progress, but it's not the end of the journey.

Making the Shift Hold

Tactical delivery creates stability by replacing reaction with coordination. But that stability only matters if it holds under pressure.

Leaders must resist the urge to overextend tactical discipline into strategic claims the system cannot yet support. The work here is simple and difficult: shape commitments deliberately and keep them.

When tactical delivery holds, chaos no longer dictates decisions. Progress here is measured by predictability. Holding this discipline is what makes learning possible later.

Coach's Note

Most leaders I talk to tell me they're in constant reactive mode, but they desire to be more proactive. It's acknowledged as the norm, and it feels impossible to change because the culture is ingrained. Pivoting quickly feels Agile, but it's just aimless chaos.

Any tactical stability they can earn satisfies the system, and that's where they get stuck. On one hand, it feels like relief. On the other, it leaves a gap they yearn to fill.

Holding tactical delivery long enough for it to become reliable is not giving up, it's responsible. But don't let complacency take root. Deliberate delivery is waiting for you.

CHAPTER 16

FROM TACTICAL TO DELIBERATE

Tactical delivery executes reliably.
Deliberate delivery decides intentionally.

Tactical delivery brings order to chaos. Incoming work is shaped before it's accepted, commitments are honored, and the organization learns how to deliver reliably. For organizations emerging from reactive delivery, this stability feels like progress, and it is.

But reliability introduces a new challenge. When plans begin to stabilize, they become easier to protect than to question. Delivery execution improves, and coordination strengthens, yet direction continues to follow established commitments and intake demand pressures. Outcomes may be referenced, but they rarely determine what continues and what stops. The system feels controlled, but it's not adapting.

Despite its limitations, tactical delivery is appealing because it can bring some semblance of order to the chaos. That order can be intoxicating, especially after years of working in reactive mode, when rhythm can start to feel like resolution. But routine does not equate to impact—it's a trap.

In the pages that follow, we'll examine the leadership decisions required to use stability deliberately, so that signals and learning can influence decisions without collapsing execution.

Orienting the Transition
Tactical → Deliberate

The shift from tactical to deliberate delivery is a shift from coordination to judgment. Planning remains essential, but what changes is what the plans are permitted to respond to.

In a tactical posture, commitments organize the system. Authority, funding, measurement, and governance reinforce adherence to what has already been agreed. That alignment restores predictability and makes execution reliable at scale. But once plans hold, questioning them feels disruptive, and signals are often confined to explaining variance rather than influencing direction.

A deliberate posture introduces examination. Assumptions are surfaced and questioned, plans are treated as provisional, and trade-offs are made explicitly. Signals and evidence are expected to inform whether existing commitments remain justified. If they're not, the system has the freedom to adjust.

At CAIP, this began with a simple question repeated for every request: "What problem are we trying to solve?"

To some, challenging solution requests felt irritating and obstructive. Alicia, the government lead, felt that tension directly. What had once been straightforward—accepting and committing to requests—now required defending why work should slow down long enough to understand the problem. That friction was the system beginning to think.

The question quickly led to another: What measurable impact does this problem have, and how would the proposed solution change it? Those answers were often unclear, and the exercise exposed how much work had been driven by assumption rather than evidence. In some cases, the answers led to requests being dropped entirely. In others, the solution approach changed once the problem was better understood.

In a deliberate posture, stability no longer serves only to protect plans—it creates the conditions to question them. Judgment determines whether the plan still deserves to continue.

How Tactical and Deliberate Delivery Show Up:

Signal	Tactical	Deliberate
Commitments	Plans are protected	Plans are tested
Ownership	Anchored to delivery	Expands toward outcomes
Learning	Explains variance	Influences prioritization
Authority	Enforces adherence	Allows examination
Behavior	Deviations are resisted	Trade-offs are visible

Establishing Deliberate Discipline

Moving from tactical to deliberate delivery is not about adding more process and control. It's about removing the insulation between execution and learning.

Minimum Viable Deliberate

Progress at this stage depends on a few conditions holding consistently:

- Outcome ownership exists for at least one meaningful problem space.

- Teams can question what's being done, not just how.

- Signals are reviewed before new commitments are locked in.

- Leadership resists re-centralizing decisions when signals and evidence create discomfort.

These shifts do not destabilize execution. They reveal that signals can influence decisions without returning the organization to chaos.

Deliberate delivery solves a specific problem: direction without examination. Assumptions are challenged, priorities are justified, and commitments are evaluated against intended outcomes.

This began to show up in how CAIP used evidence. Abandonment of the online application was not isolated. The team analyzed usage data to understand when, where, and why users dropped off. Those signals led to targeted improvements that reduced drop-off rates and increased the percentage of applications completed online.

Maria hesitated before starting the application again.

The last time, she had given up halfway through. It was confusing, and when she tried to get help, she had to start over.

This time felt different.

As she moved through the application, some of the questions were clearer. Where she had previously stopped, the process now guided her forward. She didn't have to call for help.

It still wasn't perfect. But she finished.

For the first time, she completed the application on her own.

But deliberate delivery does not yet guarantee durability. Signals may influence decisions in some areas while remaining conditional in others. Alignment improves, but reinforcement is uneven.

The risk at this stage is overcorrection.

After fighting hard to restore predictability, leaders may shield plans too aggressively or swing too far in the other direction by reopening decisions so frequently that confidence erodes. Deliberate delivery requires restraint in both directions. It's a controlled expansion of choice, avoiding a collapse back into order-taking.

Three Common Misreads:

- **Learning means slowing down**: Deliberate systems still move decisively; they just decide with better information.

- **Questioning plans undermines agreements**: Commitment strengthens when direction earns confidence.

- **Deliberateness requires full system readiness**: It can begin in one problem space without destabilizing the whole.

Deliberate delivery introduces judgment. What the organization does with that judgment determines whether learning remains situational, or if it becomes coherent across the system.

How This Transition Manifests Across the Five Dimensions

Deliberate delivery appears when signals start shaping decisions. Execution remains stable, but priorities are no longer insulated from examination. The dimensions below reveal where intentional choice is taking hold, and where tactical habits may still constrain adaptation.

Ownership and Accountability

In tactical delivery, accountability is closely tied to meeting delivery commitments. Deliberate delivery expands accountability toward achieving intended outcomes.

What Changes Here:

- Ownership becomes explicit and visible.

- Questions shift from "Did we deliver?" to "Did it improve?"

- Missed outcomes trigger inquiry rather than blame.

Deliberate ownership extends beyond completion but may still depend on leadership reinforcement rather than structural mandate. Under strain, ownership can still revert to task execution unless it's protected.

Funding, Contracts, and Continuity

In tactical delivery, funding reinforces planned execution and predictability. Deliberate delivery begins linking funding decisions to outcome relevance by scoping product spaces.

What Changes Here:

- Contracts allow measures of success to evolve post-award based on signals and supporting evidence.

- Continuity is protected to preserve learning and domain knowledge through stable product teams.

- Performance feedback carries more weight than contractual metrics in guiding decisions.

Evidence and learning gain influence, but funding structures may still resist adjustment when signals challenge existing commitments.

Measurement and Learning

In tactical delivery, measurement primarily reinforces plan adherence and delivery performance by focusing on velocity, planned vs. actual, and story points completed. Deliberate delivery allows signals to more directly influence decisions and performance by focusing on customer satisfaction, time-to-value, and domain-specific outcome measures.

What Changes Here:

- Outcomes are measured alongside delivery performance and plan adherence.

- Signals challenge assumptions and inform reprioritization discussions.

- Signals are expected to influence decisions before commitments harden.

Signals begin to shape decisions, but they may not yet carry authority strong enough to override entrenched expectations. Under scrutiny, delivery metrics can still crowd out outcome signals.

Team Authority and Decision Rights

In tactical delivery, teams execute assigned plans within predefined constraints. Deliberate delivery invites teams into trade-off conversations and shared decision-making to ensure they are delivering the next right thing, not just the next thing in the plan.

What Changes Here:

- Teams participate in problem framing.

- Recommendations influence sequencing, scope, and trade-off decisions.

- Authority expands within defined boundaries to guide decisions.

Authority broadens, but it's still conditional. Under pressure, decision rights can be pulled back up the chain.

Leadership Behavior and Governance

In tactical delivery, leadership reinforces plans, commitments, and compliance through oversight and control. Deliberate delivery reinforces signals and adjustment through inquiry and guidance.

What Changes Here:

- Leaders ask whether current direction remains justified.

- Governance creates space to review signals and impact, and to adjust as needed.

- Trade-offs are surfaced and defended transparently.

Signals begin to influence decisions, but they do not yet hold under pressure. When pressure rises, leadership behavior can revert to familiar controls, causing accountability to retreat despite stated intent.

If This Feels Familiar

If the system executes reliably but there's hesitation to revisit direction once plans are set, you may already be operating tactically at scale.

If signals are acknowledged but only occasionally allowed to change priorities, deliberateness is likely present but not yet sustained.

If leaders support learning in principle but they override signals and evidence when the heat rises, the shift you're facing is not about tools or teams—it's about whether the system is willing to trust what it learns.

If you're seeing these patterns, deliberate delivery is within reach. It's the signal that the next move is possible.

Making the Shift Hold

Deliberate delivery makes learning consequential. That shift only matters learning is protected when it becomes uncomfortable and allowed to reshape direction without collapsing execution.

Plans must remain flexible, outcome ownership must be defended, and signals must be allowed to challenge prior decisions without triggering reversion to control. When deliberate delivery holds in meaningful problem spaces, the system proves it can adapt intentionally. Progress at this stage is uneven by design, but that unevenness is acceptable only if learning persists where it matters most.

Coach's Note

Let's be honest, the real risk of allowing signals to influence decisions is that it could prove previous assumptions were flawed. Whether that's a good thing or bad thing depends on perspective.

If the system accepts that being wrong is an opportunity to improve, it's a good thing. If the culture punishes being wrong, then the tendency is to avoid it at all costs.

And it also disrupts predictability. Introducing uncertainty can feel like undoing hard-won progress. This is especially true in environments that celebrate speed and volume above all else.

That discomfort is expected and there will be resistance. Deliberateness does not feel efficient at first. It feels exposed.

If signals start to surface tension, resist the urge to smooth it over. The goal is not comfort. The goal is to deliver what matters.

CHAPTER 17

FROM DELIBERATE TO INTEGRATED

Deliberate delivery introduces learning.
Integrated delivery aligns the system around it.

D eliberate delivery begins when direction is allowed to respond to
signals, supported by evidence. Teams test assumptions, revisit
priorities, and adjust course based on what they learn rather than
defending plans already in motion. Outcomes begin to matter—not just
execution—and decisions become more intentional as signals start to
shape what comes next.

But intentionality can still depend on protection. Signals may
influence decisions in one area and not in another. Ownership may exist
here and there, but reinforcement varies. Authority aligns in one place
and retreats in another. This posture can slip because signals and
learning are still competing with older reflexes such as plan defense,
escalation, and control.

That's what makes deliberate delivery both powerful and
misleading. It can feel sufficient because it produces visible examples of
learning in action. But pockets of progress are not the same as universal
reinforcement. Until ownership, authority, and governance reinforce
learning together, it remains conditional rather than systemic.

In the pages that follow, we'll examine the leadership choices
required to move beyond protected learning and establish
reinforcement across the decision system.

Orienting the Transition
Deliberate → Integrated

The shift from deliberate to integrated delivery is a shift from local signals to system coherence. Signals and learning no longer live in silos. They become aligned across ownership, authority, and governance.

In a deliberate posture, signals can influence decisions, but only where leaders choose to allow it. Signals and learning often survive through sponsorship, pilot carve-outs, or individual credibility. When conflict rises, the system may still default to familiar behaviors: defend the plan, escalate the decision, protect alignment.

An integrated posture changes what the system expects. Outcome ownership is explicit, reviewed before decisions harden, and authority stays aligned with accountability. Trade-offs are made with data in the room as learning is no longer a discretionary activity—it becomes part of how decisions are made.

Integrated delivery doesn't depend solely on protection from a single leader. It holds because ownership, authority, and governance reinforce learning together.

In a coherent system, signals and learning don't have to fight for space. They show up consistently—in how priorities are set, how trade-offs are evaluated, and how progress is measured. Teams are no longer working to prove their plan was correct; they are working to understand whether it should continue. Decisions follow the same expectations regardless of where the work sits.

At CAIP, this shift showed up in how problems were defined and pursued. When issues surfaced in the application, they were no longer treated as isolated requests. They were traced to their impact on completion rates, processing time, and user understanding—and addressed with that full context in mind. Decisions reflected shared ownership across the system, not just within individual teams.

How Deliberate and Integrated Delivery Show Up:

Signal	Deliberate	Integrated
Commitments	Adjusted selectively	Reviewed systematically
Ownership	Exists but uneven	Designed and reinforced
Learning	Influences decisions locally	Shapes direction routinely
Authority	Situational	Explicit and stable
Behavior	Learning competes with control	Learning holds under scrutiny

Establishing Integrated Discipline

Moving from deliberate to integrated delivery is not about expanding learning everywhere. It's about making signals and learning reliable where they matter most.

Minimum Viable Integrated

Progress at this stage depends on a few conditions holding consistently:

- Outcome ownership is explicit and reinforced beyond individual leaders.

- Signals shape decisions before commitments are made and continue to guide adjustment as outcomes evolve.

- Authority remains aligned with accountability when trade-offs challenge direction.

- Governance reinforces signals and learning rather than bypassing them amidst urgency.

These shifts don't eliminate uncertainty. They demonstrate that the organization can sustain learning, ownership, and authority together because the system reinforces them.

Integrated delivery solves a specific problem: learning that only survives when protected. Outcome owners are expected to steward direction through uncertainty, treating evidence as a decision input instead of an inconvenience. But integrated delivery is not the finish line. Reinforcement still matters. If the organization relaxes the mechanisms that made learning reliable, it becomes optional again.

The risk at this stage is overconfidence.

When integration is treated as success, reinforcement can weaken. Governance may relax and learning can become optional instead of expected. Rather than a milestone to celebrate as finished, integrated delivery must be treated as an operating standard to sustain.

Three Common Misreads:

- **Integration equals optimization:** The system sustains learning, but it may not yet evolve it.

- **Durability equals permanence:** Reinforcement still matters, even after progress stabilizes.

- **Consistency equals completeness:** Some structural gaps may still remain unresolved.

Integrated delivery stabilizes learning. What the organization does with that stability determines whether it becomes normalized or erodes under pressure.

How This Transition Manifests Across the Five Dimensions

Integrated delivery becomes visible when learning is reinforced across the decision system, beyond just inside teams. Ownership, authority, and governance begin reinforcing the same direction, making learning harder to bypass when pressure rises. The dimensions below show where learning, ownership, and authority begin operating as a coherent whole, and where older patterns may still pull decisions upward.

Ownership and Accountability

In deliberate delivery, outcome ownership exists but may rely on individual credibility or sponsorship. Integrated delivery formalizes ownership and reinforces it through governance, funding, and leadership behavior.

What Changes Here:

- Outcomes have clear, durable owners responsible for improving results over time.

- Accountability persists through uncertainty rather than retreating when conditions change.

- Ownership does not regress when trade-offs become uncomfortable or outcomes remain uncertain.

Integrated ownership survives because it's structurally reinforced. Accountability no longer depends on advocacy or leadership intervention to hold.

Funding, Contracts, and Continuity

In deliberate delivery, funding allows signals to influence decisions selectively. Integrated delivery structures funding and contracts to preserve learning over time by assigning stable teams to problem spaces and allowing the flexibility to pursue evolving outcomes over time.

What Changes Here:

- Teams are funded around enduring problem spaces.

- Performance expectations evolve as understanding of the problem space deepens through signals and learning.

- Continuity of signals and learning is intentionally protected across funding cycles by maintaining domain expertise.

Funding stops acting like a reset button. Learning persists because continuity is designed into expectations rather than left to chance. Progress compounds because teams are able to build on what they've already learned rather than starting over.

Measurement and Learning

In deliberate delivery, signals support local learning but don't consistently change decisions. In integrated delivery, signals are aligned across the system and inform portfolio-level decisions. Team-level metrics connect clearly to those signals, showing how product performance supports strategic objectives.

What Changes Here:

- Outcomes are reviewed consistently across problem spaces.

- Signals consistently inform prioritization and trade-offs.

- Evidence and learning influences what continues, changes, or stops.

Measurement becomes a system feedback loop rather than a team artifact. Learning holds because evidence is expected, reinforced, and meaningful across the portfolio.

Team Authority and Decision Rights

In deliberate delivery, authority aligns with outcomes in limited areas. Integrated delivery makes decision rights explicit and stable across the system.

What Changes Here:

- Teams accountable for outcomes can shape direction.

- Leadership involvement is intentional, not reflexive, focusing on removing constraints rather than reclaiming decisions.

- Authority holds when trade-offs emerge, allowing teams to adjust direction without waiting for escalation.

Integrated decision-making keeps authority close to the information that informs it. Decisions are made where the work and evidence are best understood, rather than drifting up the chain of command. Leaders are accountable for what users and the mission achieves as a result of what the teams deliver.

Leadership Behavior and Governance

In deliberate delivery, leaders invite signals and evidence but may override it when delivery is stressed. Integrated delivery reinforces learning consistently through governance. Governance provides direction and guardrails, not explicit policy and procedure.

What Changes Here:

- Leaders remove constraints rather than absorb decisions, allowing teams to act on the information they hold.

- Governance expects evidence-informed discussion.

- Leadership behavior remains predictable under scrutiny.

Intent survives because leadership behavior no longer varies with pressure. Learning, ownership, and authority hold not through intervention, but through consistent governance and expectations.

If This Feels Familiar

If signals influence decisions in some areas but not in others, you may already be operating deliberately.

If outcome ownership holds until results disappoint, and then authority retreats, integration has not yet taken hold.

If leaders support learning in principle but it's bypassed to preserve alignment or momentum, the issue you're facing is structural, more so than cultural.

Recognizing that tension is crucial. It's the signal that integration is at hand but needs more time to stabilize across the system.

Making the Shift Hold

Integrated delivery holds when learning is no longer optional. But that only matters if signals continue to influence decisions under scrutiny.

Making this shift hold requires leaders to reinforce deliberateness consistently across the system, especially when pressure makes it tempting to revert to control. The work is not to intervene more, but to ensure the system continues to behave as designed.

Apart from policy-driven changes, signals became non-negotiable in shaping decisions and direction at CAIP. Ideas were expected to be pressure-tested. Success was measured by what changed as a result of what was delivered. These expectations were reinforced consistently across planning, prioritization, and governance. That reliability became visible in how the experience changed.

When Maria's semi-annual renewal came due, she didn't dread it.

The last time she applied, the process had improved. She could move through it on her own, guided step by step. But she still felt a quiet tension—unsure if she'd lose her progress or miss something that would send her back to the beginning.

This time, much of her information was already there.

She reviewed what had changed, updated what was needed, and moved through the process without confusion. When additional information was required, she understood why and how to provide it.

She didn't have to start over. She didn't have to call for help.

Inside the agency, Daniel no longer pieced together her application across multiple systems. The information he needed was visible in one place, with enough context to confidently make a decision.

Maria submitted her renewal knowing what to expect. And when the decision came, she understood it.

The process didn't just work. It made sense.

When integrated delivery holds, signals and learning no longer depend on protection. They become part of how the system operates—consistently, even under pressure.

What Maria experienced was not a one-time improvement. It was the result of a system that could sustain clarity, continuity, and accountability across every step. That reliability is what makes normalization possible.

Coach's Note

The shift into integrated delivery can feel easier than your previous moves because the work here is no longer to inspire change, it's to sustain it. That often brings less resistance, and for the first time, progress can feel natural rather than forced.

Getting here feels like you've made it. And in many ways, you have. Integrated delivery is a huge milestone, and you should be proud to be a part of it.

But this is also where many organizations stall and relapse. As soon as things begin to work, the urgency fades or leadership changes. Reinforcement becomes less intentional, and over time, the system starts to drift back toward familiar patterns.

Progress doesn't move in a straight line and hold. It slips, stabilizes, and often has to be fought back into place.

Celebrate the win, fight to sustain it, and keep pushing for the final posture.

CHAPTER 18

FROM INTEGRATED TO NORMALIZED

Integrated delivery reinforces behavior.
Normalized delivery makes it inherent.

Integrated delivery aligns the system around sound behavior. Ownership is clear, authority aligns with accountability, evidence informs decisions before commitments are set, and governance absorbs pressure without collapsing into escalation. The organization behaves cohesively because its decision system operates as a coherent whole.

But alignment can still depend on vigilance. Leaders must remain attentive, governance must continue reinforcing intent, and decision rights must be defended when challenged. The posture holds because those reinforcing behaviors are actively maintained.

That dependence is subtle, but real. When attention shifts, when leadership turns over, or when urgency intensifies, even an integrated system can drift if those reinforcing forces weaken.

This is the difference between a system that behaves well when it's watched and one that behaves well because it has learned how. Integrated delivery strengthens the architecture of decision-making, but the architecture still requires leaders to maintain its integrity.

In the pages that follow, we'll examine the leadership choices required to remove that dependency, so that progress persists because it has become how the organization operates.

Orienting the Transition
Integrated → Normalized

The shift from integrated to normalized delivery is a shift from reinforced discipline to ingrained behavior. Product-Led behavior becomes the default rather than something leaders must actively sustain.

In an integrated posture, learning, ownership, and authority are aligned, but are still consciously maintained. Governance reinforces discovery, leaders protect decision rights, and alignment holds because it's intentionally preserved.

A normalized posture changes what feels natural. Signals influence decisions and direction without advocacy, authority remains aligned without re-negotiation, and ownership persists across organizational transitions. The system continues to behave as designed even when no one is guarding it.

Normalized delivery does not eliminate pressure or trade-offs. It changes the response. The organization adapts without reverting to previous postures because disciplined behavior has become ingrained.

How Integrated and Normalized Delivery Show Up:

Signal	Integrated	Normalized
Commitments	Actively reinforced	Assumed and sustained
Ownership	Reinforced by structure	Persists without reinforcement
Learning	Expected and reviewed	Automatic and continuous
Authority	Explicit and defended	Exercised without re-clarification
Behavior	Product-Led behavior is reinforced	Product-Led behavior is ingrained

Establishing Normalized Discipline

Moving from integrated to normalized delivery is not about adding new governance mechanisms. It's about removing reliance on vigilance.

Minimum Viable Normalized

Progress at this stage depends on a few conditions holding consistently:

- Outcome ownership persists across leadership changes and reorganizations.

- Learning influences direction without requiring sponsorship.

- Decision authority remains aligned to outcomes without repeated clarification.

- Governance embeds inquiry as a default expectation.

These shifts do not introduce new capabilities. They demonstrate the organization behaves consistently because its decision system now sustains it.

Normalized delivery solves a specific problem: progress that depends on constant reinforcement. Learning compounds, ownership endures, and authority remains stable. But normalization is not permanence. Without attentiveness, even ingrained behavior can erode.

The risk at this stage is stagnation.

When normalized delivery is mistaken for permanence, feedback weakens. Governance grows lighter. Alignment blurs subtly rather than visibly. The system may not collapse, but it can plateau.

Three Common Misreads:

- **Consistency equals rigidity**: Normalized systems adapt continuously, without drama.

- **Low escalation equals disengagement**: Fewer escalations reflect clearer authority, not reduced accountability.

- **Stability equals stagnation**: Reduced noise enables focus and compounding improvement.

Normalized delivery removes friction from good behavior. What the organization does with that freedom determines whether progress compounds or levels off.

How This Transition Manifests Across the Five Dimensions

Normalized delivery becomes visible when learning, ownership, and authority persist without intervention. The dimensions below reveal where behavior has become institutionalized and where it may still depend on reinforcement.

Ownership and Accountability

In integrated delivery, outcome ownership is reinforced. Normalized delivery sustains ownership by default, without requiring reinforcement.

What Changes Here:
- Outcome ownership survives leadership turnover.

- Accountability no longer depends on active reinforcement.

- Trade-offs remain owned at the appropriate level without reverting upward.

Ownership no longer needs protection to survive. The system expects outcomes to be owned because accountability is encoded in roles, decision rights, and expectations.

Funding, Contracts, and Continuity

In integrated delivery, funding and contracts are designed to preserve continuity through learning and team stability. Normalized delivery sustains continuity by combining trained government staff with a balanced, cascading mix of contracts.

What Changes Here:

- Continuity persists across budget cycles, leadership changes, and vendor transitions.

- Funding no longer resets learning or ownership by default.

- Government drives domain stewardship.

Continuity stops being something leaders must defend. Learning compounds because work is no longer repeatedly reset by structural change, making improvement cumulative rather than cyclical.

Measurement and Learning

In integrated delivery, signals and learning influence decisions because leaders consistently reinforce it. Normalized delivery expects evidence to shape decisions without requiring advocacy or protection.

What Changes Here:

- Signals are acted on automatically rather than selectively.

- Evidence challenges plans without triggering defensiveness.

- Signals are trusted as a decision input rather than negotiated as justification.

Learning no longer competes with delivery for legitimacy. Signals become a stabilizing force because evidence is assumed to matter.

Team Authority and Decision Rights

In integrated delivery, decision rights are explicit but must be defended when challenged. Normalized delivery exercises authority consistently without re-clarification.

What Changes Here:

- Teams retain decision authority even during executive review.

- Authority doesn't retreat in the face of uncertainty or scrutiny.

- Leadership involvement is used intentionally, not reflexively.

Authority stops being situational. Teams act decisively because boundaries are clear and stable. Decisions remain close to the work without fragmenting alignment.

Leadership Behavior and Governance

In integrated delivery, leadership behavior reinforces intent through discipline and consistency. Normalized delivery sustains intent regardless of who's leading or present.

What Changes Here:

- Governance reinforces signals and learning without relying on individual leaders.

- Leadership transitions do not reset delivery posture.

- Oversight sustains intent rather than reasserting control.

Leadership behavior becomes institutional rather than personal. Governance protects learning as a system property, allowing intent to hold because it's embedded, not because it's championed.

Making the Shift Hold

Normalized delivery holds when the system behaves Product-Led without vigilance. That durability only matters if it persists when attention shifts and urgency rises.

Making this shift hold means removing the need to remind or rescue the system. Leaders focus less on sustaining intent and more on maintaining alignment as conditions evolve.

This posture is difficult to achieve. Leadership changes, reorganizations occur, and champions of the operating model come and go. For the shift to hold, Product-Led thinking and the supporting leadership system must be embedded deeply enough to persist through those changes.

When normalized delivery holds, progress is measured by resilience. The system absorbs pressure without reverting because it no longer depends on reinforcement to behave well.

Coach's Note

Normalization can feel anticlimactic. There's no major breakthrough, announcement, or moment where everyone agrees, "We've arrived." And that can make it hard to recognize.

If it feels less exciting, that's okay. It means the work is holding.

But don't mistake stability for permanence. This posture is difficult to reach and even harder to sustain. It's not uncommon for organizations to move close to it, only to drift when new leadership arrives, or they take their eye off the ball.

But when progress no longer depends on who's in the room… when learning continues without sponsorship… when authority doesn't retreat under pressure… something real has changed.

The goal was never to arrive somewhere new. It was to make better behavior unavoidable.

* * *

By this point, the shift should be clear. What it looks like when delivery is connected to outcomes. What breaks when it isn't. And what changes when ownership, decisions, and learning begin to align.

The next question is how to begin applying it in real work. The next section focuses on that. Where to start. What to try. What to expect as you do. And how to respond when the system pushes back. Because this doesn't begin with a reorganization or a new mandate. It begins by working differently—right where you are.

OPERATIONALIZING THE SHIFT

Deciding to become Product-Led is only the beginning. The real work is starting in a place where different behavior can take hold, learning what the system makes difficult, and creating the conditions for that change to last. This section shows how to begin operating differently—without waiting for reorgs, new funding, or permission. You don't need to do everything at once. But you do need to move with intent.

Good intentions don't drive change.

Good systems do.

How to Use Section Five

READ → TRY → WATCH → ADJUST → REPEAT

How to Use This Section

This section is meant to be used, not just read. Each chapter gives you something to try, something to watch for, and a logical next step.

How to Approach It

Read one chapter.
Try one change in your current work.
Watch what happens.
Use what you learn to decide what comes next.

What to Expect

Some ideas will work immediately.
Some will expose gaps.
Some will stall under pressure.
That's not failure. It's the system showing you what must change next.

Keep Moving

You don't need to apply everything at once.
Start small. Learn. Then build from there.

CHAPTER 19

WHERE TO BEGIN

You don't start by fixing the system.
You start by exposing it.

Progress does not begin with a plan to transform everything. It begins with a decision to work differently in a place where that change can actually take hold. Many organizations start too broadly. They choose the most visible initiative, the most strategic priority, or the area under the greatest pressure. The intent is understandable, but the result is predictable: dependencies multiply, decisions slow, and the system reasserts itself before anything meaningful can change.

Starting well requires restraint. You're creating a space—small enough to control, but meaningful enough to matter—where different behavior can operate long enough to learn.

Anyone Can Start Here

One of the most common reasons organizations delay change is the belief that it requires permission, structure, or sponsorship before anything can begin. While those things are necessary to sustain change, they're not required to start seeing the system more clearly.

A team member can ask better questions about the work they are doing. A product leader can reframe how a problem is defined. An executive can challenge how success is measured.

Each of these actions creates a small shift in behavior. More importantly, each one begins to expose something that was previously hidden. You're not waiting for the system to change. You're using your position within it to reveal how it actually operates.

Start With the Problem, Not the Work

Most efforts begin with work already defined. A request is made, a solution is proposed, and delivery begins. The assumption is that the problem is understood well enough to proceed. In practice, that assumption is rarely tested.

Starting differently means pausing long enough to understand what's happening today and what needs to change. This does not require a full discovery effort or a formal process. It requires clarity.

Before moving forward with any meaningful effort, force the work to answer a different set of questions:

- What problem are we trying to solve?
- What's happening today that makes this a problem?
- What's the measurable impact of that problem?
- What do we expect to change, and by how much?

These questions are simple. In many environments, they're also difficult to answer. That difficulty is not a failure—it's the first signal.

What You Will Notice Immediately

When teams begin to work this way, a pattern quickly emerges. The answers to these questions are often incomplete, inconsistent, or entirely absent. The problem may be described differently depending on who you ask. The impact may be assumed rather than measured.

The expected outcome may be unclear or disconnected from how success is currently tracked. This is not a reflection of the team's capability. It's a reflection of how the system has been designed to operate.

At CAIP, this became clear the first time Jeff asked a simple question during a team review: What should be different for applicants once this change is released?

The team had a clear answer for what they were building. They walked through the application changes—new fields, revised validation, and updated workflow steps. They could describe what would be delivered and how it would change user interaction. But when the conversation shifted to what would actually improve as a result, the answers became less certain.

Nothing had gone wrong. The work was progressing as expected. It's just that the system had simply never required the team to define what would change.

Start Small, But Make It Real

The goal is not to apply this thinking everywhere at once. It's to apply it somewhere real—where the outcome matters, where the problem is visible, and where there's enough space to try something different.

A good starting point has three characteristics:

- **The problem is real and observable**: Users feel it, teams see it, and leaders recognize it.

- **The scope is contained**: You can influence the outcome without needing the entire system to change.

- **There is space to make decisions**: Even if limited, there's enough flexibility to try a different approach.

Avoid the temptation to start with the highest-profile initiative. Those are often the most constrained. Instead, choose a place where progress can be made and observed. That's where learning begins.

Do Not Wait for Perfect Conditions

There's a natural tendency to wait until roles are clarified, metrics are defined, and leadership alignment is secured before working differently. That instinct is understandable, but it's counterproductive. If you wait for the system to be ready, you'll never see where it breaks. Starting imperfectly is not a risk. It's the method.

This tension showed up early at CAIP. The team had started asking better questions about the work in front of them. The questions were simple. The answers were not.

They didn't have clean metrics. They couldn't agree on a baseline. Ownership across teams was unclear. Every answer seemed to open up another dependency they couldn't fully control.

At one point, the conversation stalled. The instinct was to go define the measures properly, align across teams, and come back once everything was clearer. Jeff challenged that line of thinking with a provocative statement: "Anything worth doing is worth doing poorly."

He wasn't lowering the bar. He was acknowledging reality. Waiting for perfect clarity would have meant waiting indefinitely. The only way to understand the system was to move forward with incomplete answers and see what broke.

So, they continued. They defined the best version of the problem they could. They identified a rough measure, knowing it wasn't complete. They moved forward with work that was grounded in intent, even if it wasn't fully aligned across the system. As they did, the gaps became easier to see—where metrics didn't exist, where ownership broke down, and where decisions couldn't be made without escalation.

The system didn't change all at once. It began to reveal itself, because they stopped waiting for it to be ready.

What to Try

Start with one piece of work you're already involved in. Before moving forward, pause and ask:

- What problem are we trying to solve?

- What should be different if this works?

- How would we know?

Don't wait for perfect answers. Write down the best version you can and use it to guide the next step.

Then revisit it after delivery.

- Did anything actually improve for users or the mission?

- What did we learn?

- What should change next?

You're not trying to get it right. You are trying to see what the system makes difficult to answer.

What This Is Really About

This step is about exposing whether outcomes are understood, whether they are owned, and whether the system allows them to be improved.

When you can't clearly define the problem, measure its impact, or describe what success looks like, you're not ready to deliver—you're being asked to proceed without understanding. When no one can answer those questions consistently, ownership is unclear. When the answers don't change what is prioritized or how decisions are made, the system is not designed to respond to learning. These are the signals to pay attention to.

What Comes Next

Starting this way will raise new questions quickly.

- Why are outcomes not clearly defined?
- Why are metrics disconnected from impact?
- Why is ownership unclear or fragmented?
- Why is it difficult to change direction once work begins?

These are the questions that will guide what to do next—understand what these signals are telling you, and how to respond to them in a way that moves the system forward.

Coach's Note

People would get tired of hearing me say, "What problem are we trying to solve." And I would tell them, figure out how to answer the question, preemptively, and I won't have to ask it.

When teams first try this, they don't have the data. They're not close to the user. The work is already defined, and it can feel like the questions don't apply.

That's the signal. The difficulty in answering reveals how the system is set up. It reveals the gaps that need to be filled.

So, don't try to fix everything at once. Just make the problem a little clearer. One conversation. One assumption challenged. One measure defined. That's how the shift begins.

CHAPTER 20

WHAT YOU WILL REVEAL

The friction you encounter isn't failure.
It's the system becoming visible.

W hen you begin to work differently, even in a small way, you don't just change how the work is framed. You begin to see how the system actually operates.

The questions introduced in the previous chapter are simple. What makes them powerful is not the answers they produce, but the gaps they expose. Those gaps are patterns, and once you see them, it becomes difficult to ignore how consistently they show up.

The friction feels like resistance. The instinct is to move past it—to simplify the questions or to return to familiar ways of working so progress can continue. That instinct is understandable. It's also what keeps the system exactly as it is.

The goal isn't to push through the friction. It's to understand what it's telling you and to take the next step from there.

When the Problem Isn't Clear

One of the first things you'll notice is how difficult it is to define the problem in a way that stands up to scrutiny when people start questioning what should actually change. Ask a few people what problem is being solved, and you'll likely get different answers. Some will describe the capability that's being built. Others will describe a stakeholder request. Few will describe a clear, shared understanding of what's happening today and what needs to change. This is not a communication issue. It reveals that the work is not grounded in a clearly defined outcome.

This showed up differently once CAIP started asking better questions. The problem wasn't that people didn't have answers. It was that each answer pointed to a different outcome.

One person focused on processing speed. Another focused on reducing errors. Another pointed to improving the user experience. Each perspective made sense, but they were not aligned—and none were grounded in evidence.

That misalignment wasn't accidental. No one had been required to decide what mattered most. Until that choice was made, the work could continue, but it couldn't consistently improve anything.

What to Do Next

Do not wait for a perfect answer. Write the simplest version of the problem you can:

- What's happening today?

- Why does it matter?

- What would be different if it improved?

Put it in front of the people doing the work and the people depending on it. Expect disagreement. Use that disagreement to refine the problem until it can be understood consistently.

When You Can't Measure Impact

Even when the problem is understood, the next challenge appears quickly. When asked how improvement will be measured, the answers often point to activity. How much work is completed. How quickly it moves. Whether it meets expectations for delivery. What's missing is a clear way to tell whether anything actually improved. This reveals that the system tracks effort, not impact.

At CAIP, once the team aligned on an outcome, a new constraint appeared: the data they had didn't answer the question they were now asking.

They could see how many applications were processed and how long each step took, but they couldn't tell whether applicants were getting it right the first time. Processing times and throughput metrics could improve even if applicants were still struggling. The system showed movement, but not improvement. Without a way to see whether outcomes were improving, the team could continue delivering work, but they couldn't tell if it mattered.

What to Do Next

Start with one measure that reflects the direction of improvement. It doesn't need to be perfect. It doesn't need to capture everything. It just needs to be meaningful enough to guide decisions.

- What should increase, decrease, or become more consistent?

- What data exists today that gets you close?

- What's the current state, even if it's a rough estimate?

Establish a baseline and begin tracking movement over time. The goal is not precision. It's visibility. As that visibility improves, so will the quality of your decisions.

When Work Can't Change

As you begin to connect problems to outcomes and outcomes to measures, a different kind of friction emerges. Even when new information becomes available, it can be difficult to change direction because work has already been committed, plans have already been set, or expectations have already been established.

The conversation shifts from what is being learned to what was promised. This reveals that delivery is structured to follow a plan, not to respond to learning.

At CAIP, this tension became visible after work was already in motion. As the team reviewed early submissions, it became clear that applicants were still misunderstanding key parts of the form.

The team saw a better path—simplifying the experience rather than continuing to refine individual fields. But the work had already been defined. The release was scoped, approved, and committed.

The question shifted. Not "What would improve the outcome?" but "What can we change without disrupting the plan?"

The learning was clear. Acting on it was not. So, the team continued with smaller adjustments. The larger improvement—the one most likely to change the outcome—was deferred. The system allowed the team to learn. It did not allow them to respond.

What to Do Next

Do not try to change everything at once. Instead, create a small space where adjustment is allowed.

- Identify a portion of the work where decisions can still move.

- Use that space to test and refine your approach.

- Make changes based on what you learn, even if they are small.

At the same time, document where you cannot adjust. Be explicit about the constraints. These are not obstacles to work around quietly. They are signals that will need to be addressed if improvement is expected to hold over time.

When Ownership Is Unclear

As you work to define problems, measure impact, and adjust based on learning, a more fundamental issue becomes visible. When outcomes are discussed, it's often unclear who's accountable for achieving them.

This became visible when CAIP looked at why applications were still being returned for correction.

The issue didn't sit in one place. It spanned the application, the instructions, adjudication, and the call center. Each team owned part of the process. No one owned the outcome. When return rates didn't improve, the question surfaced: Who is responsible for fixing this?

The answers pointed in every direction. Each team had done its part, but none of them could change the result. Work continued. Improvements were made. But the outcome remained largely unchanged. Without ownership, there was no mechanism to connect the pieces or drive a different result.

What to Do Next

Start by assigning ownership for one outcome. Not at the organizational level. Not across multiple groups. Identify one person who is accountable for understanding, improving, and reporting on that outcome over time.

This does not require a formal restructure. It requires clarity.

- Who's accountable for improving this outcome?

- Do they have visibility into the work affecting it?

- Can they influence what happens next?

Ownership will feel incomplete at first. That's expected. The goal is not to perfect the model. It's to make ownership visible so it can be strengthened.

What These Signals Are Telling You

Each of these patterns—unclear problems, weak measures, fixed plans, fragmented ownership—may appear as isolated challenges. In practice, they're connected. They reflect how work is structured, how success is defined, and how decisions are made. You're not discovering new problems. You're seeing the existing system more clearly.

This clarity changes the conversation. Instead of asking how to deliver more efficiently, the focus shifts toward how outcomes are defined, how they are measured, and who is responsible for improving them. The work doesn't stop. But the way it's understood begins to change. That shift is what makes progress possible.

What to Try

Start with one piece of work you're currently involved in. Use what you've seen in this chapter to test it:

- Define the problem in a way that stands up to scrutiny.

- Identify one measure that reflects whether anything is improving.

- Create space to adjust based on what you learn.

- Assign one person responsible for the outcome.

Then run one cycle.

- What changed?

- What didn't?

- What made it difficult to answer those questions?

You're using the work to reveal how the system operates and where it needs to change.

What Comes Next

Once these signals are visible, the next step is not to address all of them at once. It's to take one of them seriously enough to act on.

The most effective place to start is with ownership. If outcomes are not clearly owned, improvement will not hold. If ownership is established—even in a small, imperfect way—it creates a focal point for everything else to align around.

The most important signal is this: if no one owns the outcome, nothing improves. The next step is to make ownership explicit—even in one place—and see what it takes to move it.

Coach's Note

When teams hit this stage, the instinct is to simplify the problem so progress can continue. They narrow the question, default to familiar metrics, and move forward with what they can control.

Don't reduce the question to make it easier to answer. Stay with it long enough to understand what's really happening.

Ask why the problem exists. Then ask why again. Keep going until the answer stops pointing to symptoms and starts pointing to how the system is actually operating.

That's where the real problem is.

If you move past it too quickly, nothing will improve.
If you stay with it, you'll start to see what really needs to change.

CHAPTER 21

START OWNING OUTCOMES

If no one owns the outcome, nothing improves.

B y this point, a pattern is clear. Problems are difficult to define, impact is hard to measure, work is difficult to change, and ownership is often unclear. These are not separate issues. They're connected.

When outcomes are not owned, everything else weakens. Work continues, but improvement becomes inconsistent. Decisions are made but not always tied to results. Metrics are reported but rarely used to change direction.

It's tempting to step back at this point and try to resolve the entire system before moving forward. That instinct is what keeps progress from starting. The next step is to take just one outcome and own it.

Start With One Outcome

Don't start with a program. Don't start with a portfolio. Do not attempt to align multiple teams at once. Start with one outcome that matters.

This should be something real. A problem that's visible. An area where improvement would make a difference to users, to the mission, or to how the program operates. It doesn't need to be the most strategic priority. It just needs to be meaningful enough to learn from.

At CAIP, this shift didn't begin with alignment. It began with a decision. The team had been working across multiple areas—form updates, validation rules, processing workflows—each intended to improve the overall experience. Progress was visible, but it was unclear what was actually changing.

At some point, Jeff, the contractor lead, pushed the team to stop expanding and to choose. Not everything. Just one outcome. They landed on a single question: What would it take for more applicants to submit complete applications the first time?

That outcome cut across everything—application design, instructions, adjudication, and support. It was visible in rework, in delays, and in call center volume. It wasn't perfect. It wasn't fully measurable. But it was clear enough to act on.

That decision changed the work. Not because the system had changed—but because the team had.

Define What Better Looks Like

Once an outcome is selected, the next step is to define what improvement means—in a way that can be observed.

- What should change?

- In what direction?

- By how much?

Precision is not needed at this point. Intent is. In many environments, the expectation is that measures must be fully defined, validated, and approved before they can be used. That expectation delays learning. Instead, define the best version of "better" you can today, and move forward.

Once the outcome was clear, CAIP's next challenge was defining what "better" meant.

The team didn't have a clean metric. There was no single report that showed how many applications were completed correctly the first time. The data existed in fragments—adjudication notes, system flags, inferred rework. Previously, that would have stopped progress. This time, it didn't.

They defined the best version of "better" they could with what they had. They estimated how often applications were being returned and used that as a directional baseline. It wasn't precise. It wasn't universally agreed upon. But it gave them something to work against.

Then they used it. As changes were made, they watched what happened. Did fewer applications come back? Were adjudicators spending less time correcting submissions?

Over time, the measure improved. But it improved because it was used—not because it was perfect at the start.

Assign Ownership Clearly

Ownership must be explicit. Outcomes often span multiple teams, systems, and stakeholders. Assigning ownership to a single person can feel overly simplistic, or even unrealistic. In practice, it's necessary.

Someone must be responsible for understanding the outcome, tracking its movement, and driving decisions that influence it. This doesn't mean they control everything. It means they are accountable for what happens over time.

At CAIP, once the outcome was defined, something else became unavoidable: someone had to own it.

Before this, the work moved across teams. The application team made changes. Adjudicators handled rework. The call center responded to confusion. Each group improved its part of the process. But no one was responsible for whether the overall outcome changed.

That shifted when Alicia, the government lead, took ownership of reducing returned applications. She didn't gain control over every part of the system. But she became accountable for understanding why applications were still being returned, and for driving decisions to reduce that over time.

The conversation changed immediately. Work was no longer evaluated by what was completed, but by whether it reduced returned applications. When it didn't, the next question followed: Why not?

Ownership didn't simplify the system. It made the outcome impossible to ignore.

Let the Team Determine How

Once the outcome is defined and ownership is clear, the next step is to resist a familiar instinct—to define the solution.

The role of leadership is not to prescribe how the outcome should be achieved. It's to ensure the outcome is clear and that the team has the context needed to pursue it.

This is where the shift becomes tangible. Instead of assigning work, you're defining intent. Instead of managing tasks, you're enabling decisions.

At CAIP, with the outcome clear and ownership in place, the next instinct was to define the solution.

Simplify the form. Add validation. Improve instructions. Any of those could have been turned into requirements. Instead, Jeff held the line. The outcome was fixed. How to achieve it was not.

The team tested different approaches. They changed how questions were worded. They experimented with reducing required fields. They looked at how guidance was presented and how adjudicators interpreted responses.

Not everything worked. Some changes had little impact. Others revealed new problems. But each iteration produced something they hadn't had before: evidence.

The work no longer followed a predefined path. It moved based on what was actually changing.

Work in a Loop, Not a Line

Owning an outcome changes how work is approached. It's no longer a sequence of steps to complete. It becomes a continuous loop of understanding, acting, and learning.

Before significant work begins, define the problem and the expected impact. After work is delivered, return to those expectations and assess what actually changed.

- Did the outcome move?

- What did we learn?

- What should we do next?

This doesn't need a new process. It needs discipline.

This changed how the work moved at CAIP. Instead of progressing through a defined sequence, the team began working in cycles. They started with an assumption: improving validation would reduce errors. They implemented changes and watched what happened.

Some improvement showed up. But not enough. So, they went back. They reviewed adjudication notes, looked at where applications were still breaking down, and adjusted their approach. Then they tested again. The work didn't follow a straight line. It moved in loops—each step informed by what had actually changed.

The difference wasn't process. It was that the outcome stayed in focus long enough for the work to adjust around it.

Expect Friction—and Use It

As ownership becomes clearer and work begins to align around outcomes, friction will increase in new ways.

Decisions may require input from areas that are not aligned. Data may be incomplete or difficult to access. Constraints that were previously invisible will become more apparent. This is not a sign that the approach is failing. It's a sign that it's working.

The purpose of this step is not to operate perfectly within the current system. It's to reveal where the system prevents outcomes from being owned and improved.

At CAIP, this is where the friction returned, but it showed up differently. The team now understood the problem. They had an outcome. They were learning what worked. But some of the changes required decisions outside their control.

In one case, simplifying a section of the application required coordination across policy, system design, and adjudication practices. The improvement was clear. The path to act on it was not.

The conversation shifted again. Not "Is this the right change?" but "What does it take to make this decision move?" The problem was no longer understanding the outcome. It was how decisions flowed through the system. That friction didn't stop the work. It clarified what needed to change next.

What to Try

Pick one outcome in your current work—something visible enough to matter but contained enough to influence.

Then run one cycle:

- Define what should change—even if the measure is a rough estimate.

- Assign one person responsible for that outcome.

- Let the team determine how to pursue it.

After delivery, pause and ask:

- Did the outcome actually move?

- What did we learn?

- What should change next?

Pay attention to what made those questions difficult to answer. That's where the system is limiting you. Repeat the cycle once before expanding.

What This Changes

When one outcome is owned and pursued in this way, several things begin to shift. Work becomes easier to prioritize because it's tied to a specific result. Conversations become more focused because they are grounded in impact. Decisions become clearer because they are informed by what's being learned.

These changes may be limited to a small area at first. That's enough. The goal is to create a working example of what different looks like, and to understand what it takes to sustain it.

What Comes Next

Owning an outcome is where the shift becomes real. It's also where its limits become clear. At some point, the ability to continue will depend on factors beyond the team. Authority, priorities, expectations, and constraints will begin to shape what's possible. These are not issues that can be resolved within the work itself. They require a different kind of change. That change begins with leadership.

Coach's Note

The most common mistake at this stage is trying to do too much too quickly.

Teams start to see the system more clearly, and the instinct is to expand—more outcomes, more alignment, more coordination.

That's where it breaks. So, keep it contained.
One outcome. One owner. One cycle.

Let it be imperfect. Let it expose gaps. Let it create friction.

You're not scaling the model yet. You're proving that it can work and learning what it takes to sustain it.

If you expand too early, the system will collapse the change before it has a chance to take hold.

If you keep it small, you'll start to see what actually needs to change.

CHAPTER 22

WHAT LEADERS MUST CHANGE FIRST

This does not move without leadership.

O wning an outcome changes how work is approached. It creates focus, exposes gaps, and connects effort to results in a way that's difficult to ignore. Then something happens. A decision sits outside the team. A priority shifts without context. A measure that matters isn't the one being reported. A change that should happen cannot move without approval. The work doesn't stop. But it stops moving the way it was.

The questions are still being asked. The learning is still happening. But the ability to act on it begins to narrow. What was working within the team starts to run into the boundaries of the system. At that point, the issue is no longer whether the approach works. It's whether the system will allow it to continue. This is where leadership matters most.

Allow Truth to Surface

The first shift is often the most difficult because it challenges a long-standing expectation: that work should begin with clarity and certainty.

When teams start defining problems more precisely and measuring outcomes more directly, uncertainty becomes visible. Assumptions are questioned, gaps in understanding are exposed, and early answers are incomplete and often change as learning occurs.

The instinct is to correct this—to push for clearer plans, more detailed requirements, and stronger commitments before work proceeds. That instinct is rooted in a desire for predictability. In practice, it suppresses learning.

Allowing truth to surface means accepting that clarity develops over time. It means creating space for teams to express what they do not yet know, and to proceed in a way that reduces that uncertainty rather than hiding it.

This shift became necessary once CAIP began working differently. They were no longer presenting fully defined solutions. They were bringing forward what they were still trying to understand—where applicants were struggling, what they believed was causing it, and what they wanted to test. That uncertainty created tension. The expectation in those reviews had always been clear: come with a plan, show how it will work, and move forward. Now the team was asking for space to learn before committing.

Alicia supported the approach. She didn't ask for a more polished answer. She asked what they expected to learn, how they would measure it, and what they would do based on what they found. That changed the conversation. The team was no longer expected to eliminate uncertainty before acting. They were expected to reduce it through the work itself.

Redefine What Success Means

What gets measured and reported shapes how work is done. When success is defined by delivery—completing scope, meeting timelines, staying within budget—teams will optimize for those outcomes. When success is defined by impact, the focus changes.

This shift is straightforward to describe yet difficult to implement. Delivery measures are familiar, widely understood, and often tied to performance expectations. Outcome measures are less precise at the start, require interpretation, and may take time to show movement.

As CAIP began working against an outcome, the definition of success became harder to ignore. In one review, the team reported that their planned changes had been delivered. The release was on schedule. The scope had been completed as defined.

Previously, that would have been enough. This time, Jeff asked a different question: Did it reduce the number of applications being returned? There wasn't a clear answer. The team could confirm what had been delivered. They couldn't yet show what had changed.

That moment changed how success was discussed. Delivery metrics didn't disappear, but they stopped standing on their own. They became context, not the conclusion. From that point forward, work wasn't assumed to be successful because it was completed. It had to show that something improved.

Enable Decisions Where the Work Happens

As teams begin to own outcomes, the need to make timely, informed decisions increases. Waiting for direction slows progress. Escalating every choice creates friction. At the same time, decisions that affect multiple teams or broader priorities cannot be made in isolation.

This tension is often resolved by centralizing decisions. While this can create consistency, it also creates delay and disconnect from the context in which the work is happening.

Enabling decisions where the work happens doesn't mean removing governance. It means being intentional about what decisions are made where and ensuring that those closest to the problem have the authority to act within clear boundaries.

As CAIP began adjusting based on what they were learning, another constraint became clear: decisions couldn't move fast enough to support the work.

In one case, the team identified a change that would reduce confusion in the application. But making the adjustment required approval across multiple stakeholders. They escalated. Days passed.

Then weeks. By the time a decision came back, the context had shifted, and the team had moved on. The problem wasn't understanding what to do. It was the system's inability to respond.

That's when leadership made a different choice. Decision boundaries were clarified. The team was given authority to make changes within defined constraints—improving how policy was expressed without altering its intent. They didn't control everything, but they no longer needed approval for every adjustment.

Within those boundaries, decisions started to move. The team could respond to what they were learning instead of waiting to be told what to do next.

Create Space for Learning

Owning an outcome requires time to understand what's happening, test different approaches, and observe results. In environments driven by delivery pressure, that time is often compressed or removed entirely.

Creating space for learning does not mean reducing expectations. It means recognizing that improvement depends on understanding whether the work had the intended effect.

This can take many forms:

- Allowing time to assess problems before and after delivery.

- Incorporating feedback from users and operations into decisions.

- Adjusting plans based on what is learned, even when it affects timelines.

At CAIP, learning began to compete with delivery pressure. After one release, the results were mixed. Some improvements were visible, but applications were still being returned due to misinterpretation of key questions.

The next release was already planned. The instinct was to keep going. Instead, Jeff made a different call. He asked the team to stop and walk through what they were seeing. Where were applications still breaking down? What patterns were showing up in returned cases?

That time wasn't scheduled or planned. But it revealed something the team hadn't fully seen before. The problem wasn't just missing information. It was how questions were being interpreted. That insight changed what they did next. The delay was small. The impact was not.

What These Changes Require

Each of these shifts can begin in small ways, but they require intent and consistency. If teams are encouraged to work differently but are measured the same way, the change will not hold. If decisions are delegated but frequently overridden, ownership will weaken. If learning is supported in principle but constrained in practice, it will not occur.

Leadership behavior sets the conditions for what's possible. When those conditions change, even slightly, the system begins to respond.

What to Try

Choose one outcome, then make four deliberate adjustments:

- Ask the team what they are trying to understand.

- Include one outcome measure in every review.

- Define what decisions the team can make without escalation.

- Create space after delivery to ask: What changed, and what did we learn?

Do this consistently for one outcome. Watch where the system pushes back—where decisions stall, where measures do not exist, or where learning is cut short. That's where your role becomes clear.

What Comes Next

When leadership creates space for outcomes to be owned, decisions to move, and learning to shape direction, progress can begin to extend beyond a single team or effort. That's where the next challenge emerges.

What works in one place does not automatically translate to another. Practices vary. Measures differ. Visibility becomes fragmented. Alignment becomes harder to maintain. The question shifts from whether the approach works to how it can be sustained and expanded. That requires something more than individual effort. It requires a way to operate as a system.

Coach's Note

Leaders often agree with this approach. They see the value of outcomes. They understand the need for better measures. And they want teams to have more ownership. But they don't always change how they respond when it matters.

They still ask for certainty when teams bring forward uncertainty. They still prioritize delivery metrics when outcomes are unclear. They still pull decisions back when risk increases. They still compress time when pressure builds.

It's not because they don't believe in the shift. They respond this way because the system they've been operating in expects it.

This is where the change happens. Not in what you say, but in how you respond when the work doesn't go as planned. That's when teams learn what really matters.

CHAPTER 23

WHAT MAKES IT HOLD

What you're asking the system to do is not owned by anyone.

You've seen what happens when problems are defined clearly, outcomes are made visible, and teams are able to adjust based on what they learn. Work becomes more focused. Decisions become more grounded. Progress becomes easier to see.

But progress depends on someone connecting what matters to the work being done, what's being learned, and what needs to change next. In many organizations, that responsibility is never clearly owned. Teams are expected to deliver. Leaders are expected to direct. But the work of keeping outcomes, measures, ownership, and decisions connected across the system is often left to chance.

That's why progress can take hold in one place and disappear in another. It's why teams can begin working differently without the system learning how to support that shift beyond a few people. What's missing is a function that helps the system hold what it has started.

When Progress Stops Holding

What works in one place does not automatically hold across the system. A single team can begin to define problems clearly, track outcomes, and adjust based on what they learn. And within that space, decisions move differently. Work stays connected to what is meant to improve.

Progress becomes visible in a way that feels tangible. But as soon as that way of working extends beyond one team, the differences surface.

Some teams define success in terms of outcomes. Others continue to work from predefined scope. Some measure what's changing. Others report what was completed. Each team is operating in a way that makes sense within its own context, but the system is no longer operating from a shared understanding of what success means.

This became visible at CAIP as teams working on different parts of the application began to adopt outcome-based approaches at different speeds. Jeff's team was focused on reducing returned applications. They had defined a clear outcome, established a directional measure, and were adjusting based on what they were learning. They could explain what was changing and why.

At the same time, another team working on a related part of the application was still operating against a fixed set of requirements tied to a scheduled release. Their progress was reported in terms of scope completed and milestones achieved. Their work intersected with the same user experience, but it wasn't being evaluated in the same way.

The difference didn't show up in delivery. It showed up when a decision had to be made. A change to the application flow required coordination between the two teams. Jeff's team wanted to adjust based on what they were learning. The other team was working against an approved plan. The question wasn't whether the change would improve the outcome. The question was whether it fit within their plan. The decision slowed because the system had no shared way to resolve it.

From a leadership perspective, the picture was just as fragmented. Progress could be seen in parts, but not across the system. Some outcomes were improving. Others were unclear. Measures didn't align. Decisions required interpretation instead of evidence.

The issue was not whether the approach worked. It was that no one was responsible for making it work as a system.

The Gap No One Owns

This is not a knowledge problem. Teams know how to define problems more clearly. They know how to measure outcomes. They know how to learn from what they deliver and adjust. You've seen that already.

It's not a capability problem either. The roles exist. Product owners, analysts, delivery leads, program managers—each touches part of this work. Each contributes to how problems are framed, how progress is tracked, and how decisions are made.

The issue is ownership. No one is consistently responsible for ensuring that what matters stays connected to the work being done, and to what is changing as a result.

Without that responsibility, each part of the system optimizes locally. Problems are defined based on immediate context. Measures reflect what's available rather than what's needed. Ownership is scoped to what can be controlled. Decisions are made with partial information, often constrained by plans, contracts, or reporting structures. Individually, these choices make sense. Collectively, they don't hold.

Learning happens, but it stays where it was discovered. Progress occurs, but it can't be explained or extended. Decisions are made, but not always in response to what's changing. What's missing is a function responsible for keeping these elements connected—continuously, and across the system.

The Function That Makes It Hold

When this gap becomes visible, the instinct is to reinforce it within existing roles. Ask teams to define problems more clearly. Ask product owners to focus on outcomes. Ask leaders to use data in decisions. Individually, these are the right expectations. They each should do those things. The issue is not what's being asked of them. The issue is what supports them in doing it—consistently, across teams, and over time.

Each role carries part of the responsibility. But no one role is responsible for ensuring that these elements stay connected as a system. So, the system reverts. Under pressure, problem definitions narrow back to scope. Measures shift to what's easiest to report. Decisions default to what was planned. Learning becomes something teams do locally—if time allows—rather than something the system depends on.

For this way of working to hold, responsibility has to become explicit. Someone has to ensure that teams have the data, signals, and shared understanding needed to define problems clearly. That measures reflect what is meant to change—not just what's delivered. That learning is visible beyond a single team. That decisions respond to what is actually happening, not just what was expected. Not as a one-time effort, but as a continuous function of how the system operates.

This is the role ProductOps for Government™ is designed to play. It doesn't replace these responsibilities. It enables them. It sits between leadership intent and delivery execution, ensuring that what the organization is trying to achieve stays connected to what teams are doing, and to what is changing as a result.

When that function is present, teams are able to define problems with clarity because the data and context are available. Product owners are able to focus on outcomes because measures are meaningful and visible. Leaders are able to make better decisions because learning is surfaced and shared.

Without it, this way of working depends on individual effort. It shows up where people push for it and fades where they don't. With it, those responsibilities become sustainable—supported, reinforced, and able to extend across the system. That's what allows progress to hold.

Making It Real

One of the most common misconceptions is that something like this requires a full redesign of how work is structured. It doesn't.

This work already exists. Every program is trying to define problems, track progress, align across teams, and understand what changed after delivery. The intent is there. What's missing is consistency, connection, and ownership across those activities.

Working Within What Already Exists

In many government programs, the responsibilities that make this hold are already distributed across roles. Each of these roles contributes to how problems are defined, how progress is measured, and how decisions are made. But none of them are responsible for ensuring those elements stay connected across the system. So, the work fragments.

This shift starts by clarifying responsibilities. In practice, this often emerges as a small, focused function, sometimes a single role at first, working across teams to:

- Align how problems are defined when they begin to diverge.

- Ensure measures reflect what is meant to improve, not just what is delivered.

- Make signals and learning visible in ways that can be acted on.

- Support teams when they get stuck between scope, outcomes, and decision constraints.

This function does not take ownership away from teams. It reinforces it by making ownership visible and sustained over time. It's less about authority and more about connection.

Working Within Existing Contracts

In government environments, what holds is shaped by how work is funded and scoped. If this responsibility is not recognized within the work, it becomes optional. And under pressure, optional work is the first thing to go.

The challenge is that most contracts already include pieces of this responsibility, but not in a way that makes it coherent. The work is there. It's just not defined this way.

Making this real within an existing contract often starts by making that responsibility explicit within the scope that already exists:

- Ensuring outcome measures are defined and used.

- Connecting discovery, delivery, and validation as a continuous improvement cycle.

- Creating shared visibility across teams for what is changing and why.

- Supporting decision-making with evidence.

This does not entail rewriting the contract. In most cases, it involves using the flexibility that already exists within it.

Building It Into Future Work

Where this becomes sustainable is when it's treated as part of how delivery is expected to operate.

In future acquisitions, this shows up in how work is described and evaluated. Not just what will be delivered, but how progress will be measured. Not just what features will be built, but how outcomes will be defined and validated. Not just how teams will execute, but how learning will inform what happens next. Just as any role or function can be written into the scope, so too can a ProductOps function for enabling and validating measurable outcomes.

When those expectations are written into the work itself, this function becomes part of how the system operates—funded, reinforced, and sustained over time.

Starting Small—But Intentionally

This does not begin at scale. It begins in one place where the conditions exist to support it. Choose an outcome that matters and that can be influenced. One where the problem is visible, a measure can be defined, and ownership can begin to take shape.

Then ensure that outcome is supported differently:

- The problem is defined clearly enough to act on.

- The measure reflects what is meant to change.

- Progress is made visible beyond a single team.

- Decisions adjust based on what is being learned.

That's enough to start.

From there, the value becomes visible in how decisions change, how progress is understood, and how outcomes begin to move. That's what allows this to extend—deliberately, and in places where it can hold.

Closing

What you've seen throughout this book is not a new set of practices. It's a different way of working—one that connects what matters to what is done, and what's learned to what happens next. You've seen how that changes the work. Problems become clearer. Decisions become more grounded. Progress becomes visible in ways that can be understood and acted on.

But none of that sustains itself. Left alone, the system returns to what it knows. Scope replaces outcomes. Reporting replaces learning. Decisions follow plans instead of evidence. Not because people choose it, but because nothing is responsible for holding anything else in place.

That's the shift this chapter completes. For this way of working to last, the system itself has to carry it. The responsibility for connecting outcomes, ownership, delivery, and learning cannot sit between roles or depend on individual effort. It has to be owned—intentionally, and continuously.

When it is, something changes. Decisions begin to reflect what is actually happening. Learning moves beyond the teams that discovered it. Outcomes become something the organization can see, understand, and improve over time. That's what allows progress to hold.

Coach's Note

Most transformations ebb and flow, progressing and regressing. Leadership attention shifts. Delivery pressure returns. The system gradually stops reinforcing the behavior it once encouraged.

What was intentional becomes optional.
What was measured becomes reported.
What was learned stops changing what happens next.

Nothing breaks all at once. It just stops holding.

Sustaining this way of working is not about reminders or renewed commitment. It requires ownership of the system itself.

When the responsibility for connecting outcomes, decisions, and learning is clearly owned, the system no longer depends on attention to maintain it. The system carries it forward.

Don't skip this part.

Final Thoughts

Product-Led delivery is not a project to complete. It's a system to maintain. When outcomes are visible, learning is routine, and authority remains aligned, improvement compounds.

That's what you saw in CAIP. The shift did not succeed because a framework was introduced or a transformation was declared. It held because the organization chose to operate differently—and reinforced the conditions required to sustain it.

Teams adjusted direction earlier. Leaders made decisions with better evidence. Work improved not through bursts of reform, but through steady reinforcement. Not because people worked harder, but because the system worked differently.

The path forward does not require starting over. It requires building on what you have already begun—expanding it where it holds, strengthening it where it does not, and aligning it with how the system operates.

Trust does not return because something was delivered. It returns when what's delivered actually improves the experience.

You don't have to start everywhere.

Start where it can hold.
Define what matters.
Measure what changes.
Decide what to do next.
Then do it again.

* * *

Now let's go deliver what matters.

STARTING POSTURE DIAGNOSTIC MATRIX

A discussion tool to help leadership teams determine where Product-Led work can begin.

For each dimension (row), mark the posture (column) that best reflects how it behaves today.

Teams may mark more than one posture per dimension if the system behaves differently across programs and products.

	Reactive	Tactical	Deliberate	Integrated	Normalized
Ownership					
Continuity					
Learning					
Authority					
Governance					

Use the descriptions on the following pages to guide how each dimension is assessed.

Understanding the Dimensions

Each dimension describes a structural condition that shapes how delivery behaves.

Ownership

Who is accountable for improving outcomes.

Reactive	Work is assigned through requests.
Tactical	Ownership is tied to projects.
Deliberate	Product ownership is emerging.
Integrated	Ownership spans outcomes and lifecycle.
Normalized	Ownership is sustained across products.

Continuity

Whether teams remain connected to the outcomes they influence.

Reactive	Teams assemble temporarily.
Tactical	Work is organized around projects.
Deliberate	Product continuity is limited.
Integrated	Product teams are stable.
Normalized	Product ownership ensures.

Learning

How signals and evidence influence decisions.

Reactive	Feedback is anecdotal.
Tactical	Metrics are collected but rarely used.
Deliberate	Signals inform decisions.
Integrated	Signals and evidence drive priorities.
Normalized	Continuous learning shapes direction.

Authority

Where decisions are made when priorities conflict.

Reactive	Decisions are escalated frequently.
Tactical	Authority is tied to hierarchy.
Deliberate	Product leaders are gaining authority.
Integrated	Decisions are close to the evidence.
Normalized	Authority is aligned with outcomes.

Governance

How oversight interacts with delivery.

Reactive	Control is compliance driven.
Tactical	Oversight is approval based.
Deliberate	Governance enables delivery.
Integrated	Governance supports learnings.
Normalized	Governance reinforces outcomes.

Interpreting the Pattern

After marking the matrix, discuss:

- Which dimension most limits learning today?

- Where do we already have the strongest ownership?

- Which problem space has the fewest structural constraints?

- Where could Product-Led behavior hold under real conditions?

- What operating space could demonstrate measurable improvement within ninety days?

- Which dimension, if strengthened, would unlock progress across the others?

ACKNOWLEDGMENTS

The ideas in this book did not emerge from theory. They grew out of years spent working alongside leaders and teams across government who believed digital delivery could—and should—produce better outcomes for the people it serves.

Since publishing *Pursuing Timeless Agility*, I've had the privilege of working with government leaders who were not satisfied with reactive, output-driven delivery. Many I worked with believed there had to be a better way to connect delivery with mission results. They gave me the freedom to explore that question with them, to challenge assumptions, and to experiment with new approaches. The model presented in this book grew out of those experiences. We learned together, tested ideas in real environments, and refined what worked.

I'm especially grateful to Bill Pratt for writing the foreword to this book. When Bill was presiding over the DHS Agile Community of Interest, he invited me to speak on several occasions. Those forums provided an opportunity to challenge common assumptions and explore new thinking about how government delivers digital services. I'm thankful for the platform he created and for his continued leadership in this space.

My thanks also go to my colleague Dave Toth, who has been a constant sounding board for these ideas over the years. Dave challenged my thinking, pushed me to clarify the models, and patiently reviewed drafts again and again.

My thanks go to the early readers who volunteered to participate in the Advance Reader Copy process and took the time to provide thoughtful feedback. Representing perspectives from both government and industry, at all levels, they helped strengthen the clarity and usefulness of the work.

I'm grateful as well to the many government and contractor colleagues who supported and encouraged me over the years—those who regularly read the newsletters, respond to posts, and champion the ideas even when I'm not in the room. Your encouragement and validation mean more than you'll ever know.

Finally, I owe a special thank you to my wife, Amanda, who endured many nights of me disappearing into my office while this book slowly took shape. It definitely was not easier the second time around.

Improving how government delivers is never the work of one person. It's the result of many people who believe the system can be better and who are willing to work toward that goal together. I'm grateful to be part of that effort.

About the Author

Jimmie Butler is a strategist and trusted advisor focused on improving how government organizations deliver digital services and mission outcomes. Over the course of a career spanning more than thirty years, he has worked across both commercial and government environments, from early-stage startups to large enterprises. After entering the government contracting space in 2010, he began helping agencies adopt more modern approaches to digital delivery, introducing Agile ways of working and stronger product management practices focused on producing measurable outcomes aligned to strategy.

He has served in program leadership and strategic consulting roles, working alongside government leaders and their delivery partners to help both industry and government organizations become more strategic, proactive, and outcome driven. Jimmie believes government is filled with talented people who want to deliver better results but often face organizational constraints that make that difficult. Much of his work focuses on helping leaders redesign operating models so teams can gain traction and produce meaningful improvement. Jimmie founded StrategiX to focus specifically on the operating models that shape government delivery. Today he partners with government leaders and their contractors to help build better government—together. He is also the author of *Pursuing Timeless Agility* and writes frequently about Product-Led strategy and delivery transformation.

Learn more at **jimmiebutler.com** and **thinkstrategix.com**.

REFERENCES

[1] Pew Research Center. (December 4, 2025). "Public Trust in Government: 1958-2025."
https://www.pewresearch.org/politics/2025/12/04/public-trust-in-government-1958-2025/.

[2] Salesforce. (2025). *Connected Government Report. Second Edition.*
https://www.salesforce.com/content/dam/web/en_us/www/documents/industries/government/Connected-Government-Report-2025-Final.pdf.

[3] Salesforce. (2022). *Connected Government Report.*
https://www.salesforce.com/content/dam/web/en_us/www/documents/industries/government/v4-Connected-Citizen-Report-e-book.pdf.

[4] D'Emidio, T., Greenberg, S., Heidenreich, K., Klier, J., Wagner, J., and Weber, T. (September 2019). "The global case for customer experience in government." *McKinsey & Company.*
https://www.mckinsey.com/~/media/McKinsey/Industries/Public%20Sector/Our%20Insights/The%20global%20case%20for%20customer%20experience%20in%20government/The-global-case-for-customer-experience-in-government-vF.pdf

[5] Partnership for Public Service. (2024). *The State of Public Trust in Government 2024.* https://ourpublicservice.org/publications/state-of-trust-in-government-2024/.

[6] Allstadt, K. and Malfara, D. (May 9, 2017). "Building a long-term customer-experience vision at the Social Security Administration." *McKinsey & Company.* https://www.mckinsey.com/industries/public-sector/our-insights/building-a-long-term-customer-experience-vision-at-the-social-security-administration.

[7] Schwartz, M. (2017). *A Seat at the Table: IT Leadership in the Age of Agility.* IT Revolution Press, p. 50.

[8] FEDWeek. (November 14, 2023). "Performance.gov Touts Link Between Engagement, Customer Satisfaction." https://www.fedweek.com/federal-managers-daily-report/performance-gov-touts-link-between-engagement-customer-satisfaction/.

[9] Office of Personnel Management. (2025). *Federal Employee Viewpoint Survey Dashboard.* https://www.opm.gov/fevs/reports/opm-fevs-dashboard/.

[10] Kohavi, R., Crook, T., Longbotham, R., Frasca, B., Henne, R., Lavista Ferres, J., Melamed, T. (2009). *Online Experimentation at Microsoft.* Microsoft. https://ai.stanford.edu/~ronnyk/ExPThinkWeek2009Public.pdf

[11] Manstof, J., Rae, J., Knight, J., and Rome, J. (November 20, 2020). "CX takes center stage: Insights from the US federal government manager survey." *Deloitte.* https://www2.deloitte.com/us/en/insights/industry/public-sector/customer-experience-in-government.html.

[12] Dave, A., Jacobs, M., Modi, K., and Tucker-Ray, S. (November 16, 2022). "Governments can deliver exceptional customer experiences—here's how," as cited from *State of the States* benchmark. *McKinsey & Company.* https://www.mckinsey.com/industries/public-sector/our-insights/governments-can-deliver-exceptional-customer-experiences-heres-how

www.ingramcontent.com/pod-product-compliance
Lightning Source LLC
Chambersburg PA
CBHW060459290526
45791CB00001B/188